C000269435

JOE FOSS, FLYING MARINE

This book has been read by the Navy Department which found no objections to its publication.

Joe Foss,
FLYING MARINE

The Story of his Flying Circus as told to
WALTER SIMMONS

EX LIBRIS

Joe Foss is shown chatting with his men before a flight. Joe and his boys worked like a well-trained backfield when they sailed into a flight of Japs, so pre-battle planning was most informal.

(International News Photo)

JOE FOSS
FLYING MARINE

THE STORY OF HIS FLYING
CIRCUS AS TOLD TO

WALTER SIMMONS

Illustrated with Photographs

BOOKS, INC.

Distributed by

E. P. DUTTON & CO., INC.

NEW YORK   1943

LIST OF ILLUSTRATIONS

Y

5

JOE FOSS, FLYING MARINE

CHAPTER I

Y

I FOUGHT JAPS FOR SIXTY-THREE DAYS IN THE SKIES OVER THE Southwest Pacific. In that time they say I shot down twenty-six planes, the same as Eddie Rickenbacker got in 1918. The incredible luck that brought me through those battles and home again, when plenty of better men died, is something that still keeps me awake at night, wondering. My number seemed to be up time and again. But always I managed to squeak through. Not a Jap bullet touched me. Malaria was the thing that finally brought me down.

For a farm kid who always liked to shoot and who ached at the very sight of an airplane, a fighter pilot's life is the most fun there is. I wouldn't trade the memory of those sixty-three days for anything. Before the war is over, I hope and expect to get some more cracks at the fellows who started this mess.

A newspaperman once summed up my story like a golf score card by stringing a few figures together. The result looked like this:

9

Date	Planes
Oct. 13	1 Zero
Oct. 14	1 Zero
Oct. 18	3 (2 Zeros, 1 bomber)
Oct. 20	2 Zeros
Oct. 23	4 Zeros
Oct. 25	5 Zeros
Nov. 7	3 (1 Zero, 2 reconnaissance biplanes)
Nov. 12	3 (2 torpedo bombers, 1 Zero)
Nov. 15	1 reconnaissance biplane
Jan. 15	3 Zeros
Total	26

I guess the story properly begins with events in the north bedroom of a little white farmhouse four miles east of Sioux Falls, South Dakota. The date was April 17, 1915, and I was born that day. That made me twenty-seven years old in 1942—almost too old to be a fighter pilot. In fact I had to do a lot of talking to get behind a gun at all. They wanted me to use a camera in a reconnaissance plane.

As a boy I roved the countryside, hiking, snaring gophers, climbing trees, and checking birds' nests. Mother says I gave her a bad moment when I was four years old by climbing to the top of the windmill and refusing to come down. She is doubtless correct. Every farm youngster does that.

I first took to the air at about seven. It was my first year at country school, and we were playing follow the leader. When my turn came to lead, I walked up the superstructure of a little bridge that crosses a creek. Below, in the middle of the water, was a little island. I jumped. The trip time exceeded expectations, and when I finally struck, one knee hit the side of my face and drove a tooth through my puss. Everybody else had sense enough not to follow.

I was out ahead another time, racing with some kids up the old highway near our place. They couldn't run very fast, and I was looking back, laughing to myself and completely forgetful of a culvert at which the road narrows. I ran off the culvert, became air-borne, and rammed right into the bank on the other side. The shock broke my right collarbone and threw my arm out of joint. This happened on Dad's birthday. He said I always did something for him on his birthday.

He was a big man—two hundred pounds and not an ounce of it fat. Neighbors respected his wrestling and boxing ability. Frequently as a young man he gave exhibitions at fairs and Fourth of July celebrations. Before settling down to farming he played in the Ringling Circus band, toured the country with his own carnival, lost money as one of the first automobile dealers at Sioux Falls, and spent a few years as an engineer for the Great Northern Railway Company. He was a fine mechanic. As a youngster I always thought he had been everywhere and done everything worth doing.

He was straight Norwegian and five years younger than Mother, who is Scotch-Irish. She inherited the forty acres on which the house stood, and after their marriage Dad bought another eighty acres across the road.

Farm life was a hard and dangerous racket. Once Dad and I were trucking big concrete tile for casing a well we were boring. As the truck was backing down a steep hill in the pasture, the brakes went out, and the truck rolled backward. In our path were some trees, a man sleeping in a car, and several farmers working with teams. Dad did the only possible thing—he cramped the wheel. Over went the truck, smashing itself to shreds as it rolled down the hill. The cab broke off, and I was trapped as it spun along like a bicycle wheel, finally crashing into a five-strand barbed-wire fence. The big tile hurtled on all sides of me. Dad got his chest crushed under the wheel.

With trapping money—once a fine badger pelt brought twenty dollars—I bought a ten-dollar horse from a junkman. The old nag was an ornery cuss, but he could run. With my younger brother, Clifford, I frequently went after the cows a mile to the west. One night an old Model T rattled by, the driver yelled, and the old horse was off. I couldn't stop him. He took the bit in his teeth and was going full throttle when we reached the gate.

I thought he planned to go through the fence, but he put on his brakes at the last moment. It was the world's most decisive stop. I managed to hold on by clutching the mane and digging in with my feet, but Cliff whizzed past my ears like a rocket and landed across a rock. It made a new joint in his arm. I had to reload him on the horse and take him home.

Mother had no liking whatever for housework. She was outside most of the time, driving horses, milking cows, doing anything a man could do in spite of her small size. Horses frequently knocked her down and gave her black eyes. That is still true—nearly every time I see her, she is wearing a shiner.

As a youngster I wasn't of much help around the farm. I was there, acting like a busy little man, but that was about all. I wanted to go fishing and hunting—things like that.

Farm work was always interfering with my extracurricular activities.

My first gun was a spring BB model. One day, when there were some well drillers in the yard, a pigeon flock came over. I fired, and down came a pigeon with a broken wing. The workmen didn't know whether it was an accident or not; neither did I. The pigeon became one of our favorite pets.

At about fourteen I graduated to a .410 gauge shotgun. Dad gave it to me. We went hunting near Howard, South Dakota, and I got my limit, which I believe was nine birds in those days. The men in the party were surprised, and it gave me the idea that I was a pretty good shot.

I can take you to all the places I've ever hunted in my life, through the broad sweep from Vermillion clear to Aberdeen and over to the east edge of the state. This is one thing I can remember better than anything else.

Dad was the best shot I ever saw. He protected his sheep against coyotes and marauding dogs with a 45-90 Springfield, one of the first breech-loading rifles, introduced in 1873. One day, though a half mile away, he killed a dog that was molesting his flock.

I mention these things because marksmanship is important in war, and good shooting isn't learned overnight. Nearly all of our successful pilots have been boys who loved hunting as far back as they can remember.

After two years of school in the country I went to the other grades in town. Then I attended high school and played the alto saxophone in the band, a good one which represented South Dakota at the Century of Progress Exposition in Chicago in 1933. The band instructor, Arthur R.

Thompson, took a liking to me and made me his right-hand man. We'd often go hunting together.

While I was a senior, Dad was killed. It was a country crossroads tragedy. He had been plowing late at night by tractor light. A rainstorm came up, driven by a heavy wind. After taking shelter under the tractor for a while, he decided the rain would continue and started home. On the way his car ran across a high tension wire which had been brought down by the wind. The motor stalled. Dad got out to investigate and was electrocuted. I drove in from town a few minutes later, but they wouldn't let me see him.

It was the one big tragedy of my life. In this world today we could use plenty of real men like Dad.

In the fall of 1934 I enrolled at Augustana College in Sioux Falls. College wasn't much fun—I was running the farm then and had to jump into the car after classes and tear home to work. At the end of the year a college education seemed totally unnecessary, and I quit.

The next year I was a farmer. It was a disastrous dry season, and I barely got my salt back. I wound up the year working for fifty-one cents an hour at the Morrell packing plant in Sioux Falls.

Pretty soon money was jingling in my pocket again, and my eyes had been opened by seeing how hard an uneducated man had to work for a living. I decided on a college education for sure.

On the way back out to Augustana I walked past Sioux Falls College, which is near by. A fellow I knew was mowing the lawn. "Hi, there, where are you going?" he yelled. "I'm going out to register at Augustana," I said. "Why don't you come here?" he asked. "Do you think you could get me a

Joe Foss was born in this frame farmhouse, four miles east of Sioux Falls, South Dakota.
(Chicago Tribune photo)

Here is Joe (right) with his brother, Clifford. Joe was about two-and-a-half years old when this picture was taken and Clifford was twenty months younger.
(Chicago Tribune photo)

Hunting was a favorite sport with the Foss family. This picture was taken in 1930, after a successful pheasant hunt. Left to right: Flora Mary, Clifford, and Joe Foss, and a friend, Betty Lieb, now Mrs. W.W. Tyler, of St. Louis, Mo.

Dakota farm life was a hard school, but it conditioned Joe for the job he had to do. This is Clifford Foss feeding stock.

(Chicago Tribune photo)

job?" He could and did. The next thing I knew, I was a janitor boy at Sioux Falls College.

I played football there, ran distances on the track team, and went out for boxing. In the Golden Gloves tournament I had a little bad luck. A few ounces too heavy for one class, I was pushed up into the next and was the lightest man. My first bout was with a tough cookie named Mel Anderson, from Huron, South Dakota. He wound up as champion of the class. In our fight he gave me a real working over and broke my nose. It made me sore as hell when they threw in the towel, but I felt better when it developed I'd been licked by the champ.

Next day in speech class I had to give a talk. The subject concerned wrecks the airlines were having in those days. I pointed out ways by which these disasters could be avoided.

This was what was known as a "heckle" session. Anybody had a license to ask questions after the speech was over. One fellow that I didn't like any better than a snake arose and sneered, "Mr. Foss, when it comes to averting disasters, just how could a disaster of the type you encountered the other night in the ring be averted?"

It burned me. "Well, Jim," I said, "as far as I can see, the best way is to begin right now by practicing on boobs like you." And I started down from the platform after him. The class nearly broke up in a riot, but I got an A for the speech.

My interest in aviation went back a long way. Dad talked for years of buying a light plane but never had the money. In 1927 he bundled the whole family into a car and took us to Renner Field, five miles north of Sioux Falls, to see

Charles A. Lindbergh and the *Spirit of St. Louis*. I was up there in the front row and got myself an eyeful.

In 1930 a squadron of Marine planes commanded by a Captain Jerome came to town for an air fair. It was the first time I ever saw formation flying. The roar of those old egg beaters, the dust and excitement, the skill of the flyers— all those things drove me wild. That squadron leader is now Colonel Jerry Jerome, incidentally, and he is acting director of Marine aviation at Washington.

It was 1934 before I got my first ride in a plane. She was an old bucket of bolts, strung together with baling wire, but the thrill was genuine and unforgettable. In 1937 I was standing around downtown one night and heard some fellow blowing about what an aviator he was—he'd had eight hours in the air. I thought, if that guy can fly, so can I. Next day I made inquiries and found it cost sixty-five dollars to learn to solo.

At that time I was making sixty-five dollars a month working in Roy M. Tollefson's filling station and played in the municipal band on the side. This brought in forty-eight dollars a month and sometimes more if we had extra jobs. I paid sixty-five dollars, and Roy Lanning, who now instructs Army flyers at Lakeland, Florida, taught me to solo in a Taylorcraft.

Plane rental was six dollars an hour. Every time I got some cash after that, I'd rent a plane, fly out to the farm, swoop down and wave at the neighbors.

In 1939 I registered as a junior at the University of South Dakota in Vermillion. Louie Lass and Charley Stark gave me fifty cents an hour for sweeping out their meat market and working around the shop. They were two swell guys.

I waited tables and washed dishes at Sigma Alpha Epsilon fraternity house for my board and room.

Getting through school wasn't easy. My grandmother had left me twenty acres of land, which I sold for one thousand dollars to brother Cliff, who got a rare bargain. That money helped. But it was necessary to sell my car too.

In my senior year some of us worked hard to start a Civil Aeronautics Administration course and finally made it. Besides the seventy-two hour ground school, there was about fifty-eight hours of flying at Rickenbacker Field near Sioux City, Iowa, thirty-five miles away. After school we'd all jump into a car and head for the airport. Often I hitchhiked down there earlier to get in extra time. Ed Graham ran the field, and he is still there. Years ago the place was a race track, and it was there Eddie Rickenbacker won some of his first races.

I was pointing for Marine aviation—a tough thing to get into. In February, 1940, with five dollars in my pocket, I hitchhiked to Minneapolis, Minnesota, about three hundred miles away, to apply for enlistment. With me was Ralph Gunvordahl from Burke, South Dakota. He was later famous as one of the Flying Tigers over Burma. Out of twenty-eight men who applied that week end, we were the only ones accepted. Later we hitchhiked home through a snowstorm, our eyes still dilated from drops that had been put in them.

In June, after graduation from the University School of Business Administration, I reported at Wold-Chamberlain Field at Minneapolis for preliminary training. It didn't seem necessary to tell them about the hundred hours of flying time I already had. They might have thought I was a wise guy, anyway. The training took us to the stage where we could solo in a light plane and ended with about twelve hours of actual flying.

After a month's furlough spent at home I hitchhiked to the naval air station at Pensacola, Florida, making the trip in three days on $6.87. After seven months of training, I was commissioned a Marine second lieutenant March 15, 1941, and got my wings March 29.

The nine months that followed were long and distressing. I was put in a primary squadron as instructor. Once when I gave a student a cut gun we went into a spin, almost hit another plane, and dove into the ground. Both of us were covered with black and blue marks. That taught me to stay wide awake. But it wasn't till much later that I realized an instructor learns much more than he is able to teach.

On January 1, 1942, I was relieved of duty as an instructor and sent to photography school for four months at Pensacola. After that, and a promotion to first lieutenant, I was ordered to San Diego, California, and put into a reconnaissance squadron.

For six weeks there was little flying. I wanted to fight, and reconnaissance planes have no guns on them. When I kept yelling, a major said, "You're too damned ancient, Foss. Do you realize you're twenty-seven years old?" But finally they sent me to an aircraft carrier training group, where I got in a hundred hours and left with a good recommendation.

I went back to the reconnaissance squadron. One day the colonel called up and asked, "How'd you like to get in a fighter squadron?" "I'll be right up," I said. On August 1 I went in as executive officer of VMF 121 at Camp Kearney, California.

Things moved fast after that. On the ninth I was married, at Lajolla, California, to June Shakstad of Sioux Falls. We had known each other ever since high school days. On the eleventh I was promoted to captain, and by the thirtieth we were on our way to the Southwest Pacific somewhere.

CHAPTER II

Υ

WE WERE ON OUR WAY, SURE ENOUGH, EVEN IF WE SPENT
two days waiting after wives and relatives had said the last,
uncertain good-byes. On September 1 the voyage actually
started. We were on a transport—a squadron of forty Marine
pilots among thousands of troops.

Four of us were in one stateroom. With me were Colonel
Chauncey (Bud) Burnette, a humorous, mustached officer
who had formerly managed the Detroit municipal airport;
Major Leonard K. (Duke) Davis, of Coronado, California,
our squadron commander, an Annapolis man, small, witty,
and good-natured; and Lieutenant Rodney K. (Doc) Peterson, of Madison, Wisconsin, a medico.

Day after day our convoy plowed southward through the
Pacific. For most of us it was a pleasure cruise, memorable
for the friends we made, the games we played, and the
electric tension which ran through everything. We talked
aerial fighter tactics by the hour after boning up on Lieutenant Commander Jimmy Flatley's *Fighter Doctrine,* an

20

information-packed little manual about as big as three chapters of this book. We discussed the merits of various planes, debated what little we knew of the Japanese pilots, and played poker. At this game I was not unlucky.

VMF 121—the "V" stands for heavier than air, "MF" for Marine fighter—was lucky to have the Duke for its commander. He was easy to get along with; he wasn't the worrying type. Actually, he never seemed to be concerned except about one thing. That was the welfare of his boys and whether they were getting a good deal consistently. They returned his consideration by producing results another type of commander could not have got from them.

His sixteen-plane squadron (a squadron is supposed to have from eighteen to twenty-seven planes, but only sixteen operate at any one time) was organized in two flights, one of which was in my command. My assignment was also to serve as executive officer for Duke. I could see already it was going to be a good job.

The boys in the flight were as diverse as you would find in a day's hard travel, and they came from almost every section of the country. Lieutenant William Marontate, twenty-three, was from Seattle, Washington—a brash youngster who had never been intimidated in his life. He said or did what he pleased, regardless of who was around. Well-built, he was soon given the nickname "Guts" from a habit he had of inflating his belly and protruding it amazingly.

From the other end of the country came Lieutenant Oscar Bate of Essex Fells, New Jersey. Because he was a Yale graduate and had studied law at the Harvard Law School for two years, he was known as the "Legal Eagle." His middle name was Mortimer—a circumstance which called for a due share of caustic comment. Bate praticed his law on the entire outfit, constantly picking friendly arguments and upholding his position with unlikely technicalities.

Joe Palko, a master technical sergeant with wings, was also from the East. His home was Hazleton, Pennsylvania, and he was proud of his "Hunky" ancestry, as he called it. He contributed much humor with his double talk and strange imprecations in some foreign tongue. "Captain Foss," he often promised solemnly, "when this war is over, I'm going to take you back and introduce you to the entire Fordham football squad."

The other four men came from the great middle part of the United States. Two were Minnesotans—Lieutenant Koller C. Brandon, twenty-three, of Deer River, called "Casey" because of his initials, and Lieutenant Cecil (Danny) Doyle, twenty-two, of Marshall, a little fellow, always full of life, wisecracks, and raspberries for the other fellow. Brandon and Doyle were close friends. They were also the bridge champions of the ship, winning more because of their continual disconcerting chatter than from any knowledge of the conventions.

Lieutenant Thomas Furlow, twenty-three, from Ogden, Arkansas, was a good-looking, dashing flyer whose nickname, "Boot," was hung on him by Danny Doyle after they had kicked it back and forth between themselves for weeks. It was used in the naval sense when either made what the other fancied was a dumb play. Lieutenant Roger Haberman, twenty-eight, of East Ellsworth, Wisconsin, was irreverently called "Uncle," because he was elderly and serious minded—in a unique way. Among these youngsters of twenty-two and twenty-three, Bate, Haberman, and I rated

as "old men." They usually called me, in less formal moments, "Old Foos."

The food was good aboard ship, and I followed a lifetime
motto: "Eat while you can." The days had a tendency toward
monotony, but it wasn't bad. I read, made out watch lists,
enjoyed the flying fish, listened to the slightly sour concerts
of the ship's band, and occasionally served as officer of the
day. Corporal Barney Ross, the former champ who turned
out to be one of the big heroes of Guadalcanal, was on
board and put on a good show whenever he could find
sparring mates.

I got good and red from playing shuffleboard on the sun
deck in swimming trunks. Colonel Burnette and I made up
a winning combination.

Sometimes it rained and we had a fresh water shower.
Otherwise water was limited to a bucketful a day for the
four of us to use in shaving and personal cleanliness. The
ship blacked out early each evening, and our quarters were
somewhat stuffy with the portholes battened down.

Duke and I knew we were bound for Guadalcanal, but
none of the other boys in the squadron did. It was fun to
listen to them guessing. After two weeks at sea we sighted
land. Planes zoomed us, and we pulled into a South Pacific
harbor about three o'clock the afternoon of September 14.

I happened to be officer of the day, with Haberman as my
assistant, and it was a job to keep discipline among all those
boys wanting to go ashore. Haberman carried out my orders
to the nth degree—he even stopped a colonel who was
trying to go ashore.

We did get to see something of the island, rising 2,200
feet straight out of the water, but not much. There really

wasn't much to see. Mostly we languished aboard ship. It was a welcome change when we got underway again, on a new course, after three days in port.

We lost a day crossing the International Date Line. "Doc" Peterson did a carving job on me one day, spending thirty-five minutes removing a ganglion growth from my knee cap. The thing dated back to the time I spun in at Pensacola. The weather was cloudy and—believe it or not—cold. We had boat and fire drills and once sighted a big convoy.

Everyone was in good spirits as we approached our destination. Many of the boys were writing letters home for mailing the next day. Months afterward I saw the letter Casey Brandon wrote to his parents, Mr. and Mrs. Herman T. Brandon. None of us could have expressed it better.

Journey's end tomorrow, and it has certainly been a wonderful trip, in contrast to our fondest expectations. I got quite a kick out of standing near the bow of the ship and looking through binoculars at the waves breaking against the sides. It's just like looking through a kaleidoscope; you shake it and it forms a new pattern, only here the pattern keeps changing endlessly.

The water is bluer than blue out here, bluer than anything you can imagine, a beautiful blue becoming grayish black near the horizon. The ocean is boring in its nothingness by day, but a mysteriously frightening wonder at night with its shroud of speckled darkness overhead, and the moon showing through. It's comforting to lean over the rail in the silent rippling darkness and look unseeingly into the beyond, but your thoughts soon start drifting back across the sea, and then you must return indoors where there is light and gaiety and laughter. . . .

Then, on the twenty-second, we steamed into the harbor and stayed aboard waiting orders.

Rumors came to us. Things were going badly—very badly —in the Solomons. Lieutenant "Red Dog" Kendrick, San Francisco, a dashing redhead I had met in the aircraft training group at San Diego, was having good luck shooting down planes. He was killed later.

By this time all the boys had a good hunch where they were going. We transferred aboard one of the President liners, and our baggage was cut to one suitcase and a bedding roll. It hurt to leave the rest of our things behind, but at least this was a general warning that we'd see action soon.

We sent out working parties to set up our camp three miles out. We named it Camp Geiger, after Major General Roy S. Geiger, the Marine air commander. I pulled the stitches out of my knee and went to the dentist to get a cavity filled. We spent a lot of time playing They Satisfy, a sudden-death form of poker. We heard our boys at Guadalcanal had shot down thirteen Jap planes in a single day. The rest of the time we just stood by to stand by.

On the twenty-ninth we embarked on a converted carrier to be catapulted off. It was the first time any of us had been catapulted, yet there was only one accident. The hooking gadget broke when it was the turn of Lieutenant Robert F. Simpson of Chicago. His plane skidded overboard. You've seen pictures of such an accident—the pilot climbed out of his cockpit onto the wing, then took to his Mae West when the plane sank. Well, it was the pictures of this incident you saw. A photographer was on hand alert enough to catch the whole thing. A crash boat, which always stands by when planes are catapulted, picked Bob up.

Later there was another accident unconnected with us. A scout bomber dove into the water, and the plane sank.

The gunner climbed out and was saved, but the pilot drowned.

We flew our new planes to a field and worked over them like fanatics to see that every last thing was just right.

Big Bill Freeman had a piece of bad luck—he ground looped while landing behind me in a mean cross wind. Blown off the runway, he somehow got past a row of parked planes, nicked some oil barrels with one wing, and wound up against a rock pile.

Bill came to me, ashamed and downcast, and reported, "Captain, I've wrecked a plane out there." He seemed to expect a sharp bawling out—something that certainly wasn't in order under the circumstances. I sympathized with him, and he seemed disappointed. He went to the Major. "Sir, I doped off and ground looped a plane," he said. "Yes," Duke replied, "that's sure a tough wind out there."

Freeman said nothing more. He walked away and started rebuilding that plane himself. Both wing tips were damaged and the landing gear was knocked off, which is plenty to happen to any airplane. But Freeman fixed it. He'd get up at dawn, and we'd see nothing of him till after dark. All the help he had was from some fellows who did some of the heavy lifting. Before we were ready to leave, his plane was in perfect shape again. Where did he get the parts? He went to the bone yard and salvaged pieces from the wreckage!

Five of the boys from the squadron were flown to Guadalcanal about this time, but the rest of us stayed in our back-to-nature camp out in the sticks, beside a little fresh water stream. After each day's work, the eight of us from my flight peeled off our sweaty clothes and took a refreshing swim. Then, after supper, we sat around the campfire, telling stories and sometimes discussing the future. Occasionally all conversation stopped, and the men sat silently staring into the flames. I knew what they were thinking. That was my cue to launch into a story and try to snap them out of it.

Daily we got the late dope from Guadalcanal, where the Marines had landed August 7. More than anything else we were interested in reports on the Japanese Zero fighters, about which we had heard almost everything and didn't know what to believe. Those were the days of the big Zero scare. Stories about the Zero's climbing ability, its speed and maneuverability, seemed almost fantastic. But even admitting all these things were true, we saw no grounds for discouragement. We knew our planes had many virtues. We also had confidence in our long tactical training, which was and is better than the Japanese. Our hands—to put it in language a bit overstuffed—were trained to make guns destroy anything our eyes could see.

We knew the boys on Guadalcanal needed us. The landing there, true enough, was preceded by effective bombing of enemy airfields and installations all down the line. Carrier-based naval planes had supported the attack and occupation of Henderson Field, on the north side of the island. But two weeks of work were required to finish the field, which the thoughtful Japanese had brought to about 85 per cent completion for us. The Marines on the island were therefore without land-based air support until August 21.

After that, they got increasingly effective help, though the situation was still extremely tight. For a long time we owned the airfield and little else on Guadalcanal.

We were busy with test hops, dives, and strafing attacks. It rained and rained. For a while we had to hitchhike to our field. Once we got a ride with a Negro driving a truckful of rock. Later we got two jeeps. The chow was very poor. Our mouths watered October 1 when we thought of the duck and goose season opening back home. The only consolation was that the Jap season was soon to open for us.

One day I took an eighteen-plane flight on a hop to the north. The boys kept wretchedly poor position, and I reprimanded them angrily. It made me mad to think we were so close to the real thing and could be so sloppy. But the next day they snapped out of it and did a beautiful job. I felt better.

The day came when we heard that Lieutenant George A. Treptow of Chicago, one of the five boys who had gone ahead, was dead at Guadalcanal. Later we learned that his oxygen mask apparently had got out of adjustment at high altitude, and he had crashed without ever knowing of his danger.

October 6 arrived. We went aboard the carrier again, knowing this was no suitcase drill, and pulled out of the harbor. Next day, bound for action at last, we were up at 4:20 A.M. and stood by all day in case of an alarm. There was none. We checked our planes again and again.

The carrier nosed onward toward Guadalcanal, and we were up at 4:20 again. There was a "bogey"—an American plane appeared. We were edging into the hot zone, and everybody was on edge. All day we played cards without seeing the spots, and listened to the phonograph without hearing music.

CHAPTER III

Y

THE NEXT MORNING WE WERE UP AT FIVE, HAD BREAKFAST
and packed. We took plenty of pogey bait—candy—and cigarettes for the boys on Guadalcanal. Some of us were on the
list to fly over water to Henderson Field, while others, due
to a shortage of planes, were to come in later by transport.
A few of the men left behind actually had tears in their eyes.

The take-off at 12:55 P.M. was ideal. I'm not superstitious;
I flew Number 13. Looking backward and down, we saw
the deck of the receding carrier, ruled off like a ping-pong
table. Our heavy Grumman Wildcats, stoutly gunned and
armored, painted ocean blue on topside, sky blue beneath,
purred along contentedly. A few hours later we could see
Guadalcanal. The boys had doubted my navigation, but
fortunately it was right on the nose. We had hoped for a
few enemy planes; there was none in sight. All we could
see was the luxuriant, peaceful green of the island, set
jaggedly in the sea.

It was so beautiful that war and bloodshed seemed impossibly far away. Coconut palms waved politely at us, cows drowsed in the green meadows, and swimmers were splashing in a little creek.

When we neared Henderson Field, however, things looked different. We could see hundreds of pockmarks left by bombs and shells. Besides the craters, there were foxholes and slit trenches, and many wrecked planes ranged around the field, which itself was a mere cow pasture hacked out of the jungle.

Rough-looking fellows with beards came running out of the woods to meet us. They cheered almost hysterically, climbed onto the Wildcats, and seemed almost ready to kiss us. Major John L. Smith, the famous Marine ace from Lexington, Oklahoma, drove out in a jeep to say hello. Then he took us down a peg or two by pointing out that we had landed on the bomber strip. We had to take off again and land on the fighter strip, three-quarters of a mile away. There, at one of the ready tents, we met Captain Marion Carl, of Hubbard, Oregon, who was runner-up to "Smitty" in number of planes shot down.

Veteran pilots showed us to our camp—a few tents in the grove opposite the jungle. As green newcomers usually do, we secretly felt we were pretty good, but lost that cocky feeling completely after talking for fifteen minutes with the boys who had been through the mill. What dampened us most was the replies we got to questions about old friends. Several of them were dead or missing.

We were warned to expect shelling from the sea during the night. The warning was no joke, and neither was the shelling. Old-timers called it light, but the noise, intensified by the answer of our artillery, kept us awake nearly all night. Nothing fell close to us, however.

Next day was the saturnine Smitty's farewell to Guadalcanal. His boys of Fighting 23 wrote a good ending for themselves. Ordered to protect formations of torpedo planes and dive bombers in an assault on enemy shipping to the north, they were accompanied by another squadron of fighters led by Major Bob Galer of Seattle, Washington. Smitty and his men closely followed the torpedo planes as they skimmed the sea, looking for Jap ships. From above, a group of fifteen float-type Zeros saw them and dropped down in a savage attack, mistaking the wicked Grummans for torpedo bombers.

Out ahead, Major Smith gleefully noted this error and gave orders to capitalize on it. The Grummans split away from the formation and shot upward. Realizing his mistake then, the Jap leader turned his planes away, foolishly exposing their bellies.

"Give 'em something to remember our last day," Smitty told his boys, and they did. They swept through the enemy formation like a hurricane through dry leaves. Nine of the fifteen Zeros were sent burning into the sea below. The torpedo planes and dive bombers succeeded in hitting a couple of Jap ships.

Smitty racked up a score of nineteen victims in his six weeks on the island, and Captain Carl wasn't far behind with sixteen.

In the afternoon we went on our first mission—escorting bombers up the groove. We flew as high cover, then swept down, but did no strafing. I saw one of our bombers score a hit on a destroyer. There was a big explosion, blowing a lot of junk off the stern. Then I went into a cloud and didn't see whether the destroyer sank or not.

We scrambled next day when twenty-seven bombers and twenty-four Zeros approached the field, coming from their base on Bougainville Island, 260 miles to the northwest. Rain had poured down all morning, but now it was clear. After sparring around a little, the enemy fluked out on his attack, dropping the bombs two miles from the field and behind his own lines. It amused us to imagine what the Jap infantrymen thought when bombs from their own planes came raining down on their heads.

Our outfit got two bombers and a Zero. Galer's boys brought home seven bombers and four Zeros. We lost, for a little while, our first man—Lieutenant Art (Chongo) Nehf, of Phoenix, Arizona, son of the famous New York Giants' baseball pitcher. He was in Duke's flight. Coming in he ran out of gas and landed in the ocean back of the lines. Some Marine raiders went after him and later brought him back with a bad cut over his eye.

Ground troops pushed the Japs back across the Matanikau River that day.

The night was another wakeful one—there was a terrific naval engagement off Cape Esperance, the northwest hump of the island. In the morning the water was covered with heavy oil and filled with debris and swimming sailors—both American and Japanese. Boats were busy picking up survivors among the wreckage. It was much later before we connected the battle with the story of the light cruiser *Boise.* This ten-thousand-ton warship, armed with only six-inch guns, was instrumental in sinking six enemy ships in thirty minutes that night. The Japs lost two heavy cruisers,

Ready to be a Marine pilot, Joe Foss looked like this when he was commissioned a lieutenant.

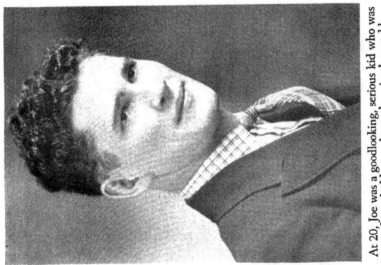

At 20, Joe was a goodlooking, serious kid who was ready and able to take a place in the world.

(Chicago Tribune photo)

Here are some of the Grumman fighters piloted by Joe Foss and his flying circus in their South Pacific battles.

(International News Photo)

a light cruiser, and three destroyers. Our chief losses were
a destroyer and 107 officers and men from the *Boise*—which
thereupon became famous as the "One Ship Navy."

Despite their licking at sea, the Japs succeeded in landing thousands of troops on the island that night.

Again I saw a bomb hit on a destroyer. It is not a bad
sight to look at. Eighteen of us got up at 4 A.M. and took
off before dawn up the channel, escorting dive bombers
assigned to chase away Jap ships remaining from the naval
action. The bombers caught two Jap destroyers just off the
coast of New Georgia—two little black splinters far below
on the water. Decoying anti-aircraft fire away from the
bombers, we saw a destroyer hit squarely, aft of amidships.
There was a great belch of smoke and flame which died away
slowly. Then the ship started burning fiercely. Torpedo
planes at the same time attacked a cruiser and left it sinking.

We didn't lose anybody, though one burst of AA fire went
right between our first and second sections, shaking up two
of the boys. (Perhaps I should explain there are two fighter
planes in a section, four in a division, and eight in a flight.)

The night was quiet. We really slept after that day's
work.

American transports landed fresh troops in the morning.
Bombs falling early on Henderson Field gave the ground
crews some holes to fill up. We went up to meet the first
enemy formation—twenty-two bombers—but failed to make
contact. We could see them, too far away, gleaming silver
against the cloudy blue sky, our anti-aircraft bursts puffing
out beneath them. Bombs also fell on the beach, killing
three of our men and wounding three others.

Two hours later came another attack—by eighteen bombers this time. As my flight climbed into position I felt excited and good, like a kid waiting for a big dish of ice cream. We climbed to the left of the big fellows before seeing five or six Zeros off to the right. I led my boys along the edge of some clouds, hoping the Zeros wouldn't see us.

In my excitement I guess I forgot to turn the radio on. Or maybe it wasn't working. Anyway, one of my boys flew alongside, waved urgently, looked up, and pointed. Thinking he was pointing at the Zeros we'd already seen, I smiled and waved back.

The first thing I knew my wingmen were gone. Attacked from above by a swarm of other Zeros, they had dived out of formation, and a Zero which had been hiding on top of the clouds was on my tail, sending a sizzling stream of tracers a few inches from my head.

The speed of his dive took him past, and he pulled up directly in front of me. I pulled up after him, got him squarely in the sights, and gave him a light burst. With a great flash he blew into a thousand pieces. It was my first Zero.

I was conscious of a lot of things—my hair standing up, a dryness of the mouth, and a crazy desire to stand up in the cockpit and yell. That's the way you feel when a Zero blows up right in front of you.

But there was other business waiting. Pulling up to get this Zero had made me a setup for three others which now came in viciously, their guns blazing. As I pushed over into a dive I saw oil fly from my oil cooler, and a hunk of wing ripped out by a cannon shell. As I dove, the motor burned out in a flash and the pistons stuck. The propeller, however, kept windmilling.

Those Zeros chased me right to the edge of the field, and I didn't dare slow up for an approach. I came in like a rocket ship, sideslipping desperately at the last moment. The landing was so hot an ambulance was called out to pick up the pieces—if any. But by some miracle I managed to stop before running into the river or the stump patches at the edge of the field. I hooked a ride back on the side of the ambulance.

The old-timers laughed when I told them what had happened. "Bet that makes a Christian out of you. You won't pull that stunt again," they chuckled.

I didn't argue. I was a sad sack that night. True, I had my first Zero, but had make a boob out of myself getting him. The rest of the boys all came back, nicked and sore. They had been sprayed good, too. Our score was three bombers and four Zeros for the day. More important, we had all learned some good lessons.

I learned mine so well the boys were soon calling me "Swivel-neck Joe." The lesson was never get so intent on pressing home your attack that you fail to look around.

Lieutenant William (Big Bill) Freeman, twenty-five, from Bonham, Texas, learned something the same day. Slow, drawling, strong as a horse, and wise in the mysteries of engineering, Bill got separated from the flight led by Major Davis. Seeing a Jap bomber formation below, he went down alone to knock out the leader of the V formation.

In a way, Bill was successful. He got the leader all right, but in doing so he gave every side gunner in the formation a swell target. They laced him from all angles. He came down convinced the attack should be started at the rear of the formation and moved progressively up. We all took Bill's lesson to heart.

Bill later flew with my outfit. He was one of thirteen men who did at one time or another. I've worked with a lot of fellows and met a lot of people, but I've never encountered a gang with such spirit. They were a team out to win, and they just couldn't be beaten. Duke Davis had a tremendous lot to do with that.

Mentioning the fact that thirteen men flew in our flight reminds me of another circumstance. I got my first Zero that day, October 13, flying the Number 13 Grumman I'd brought in from the carrier four days before. Only by that time it had been renumbered. We made it Number 53, because there was already a Number 13 among our fighters.

Japanese land-based artillery, smuggled onto the island somehow within the last few days, completed our discomfiture at 5:30 P.M. by shelling us for the first time. In the distance we could hear a faint pop, then a whistle, getting louder as the shell approached, and finally an explosion. Our destroyers and land-based artillery answered, and finally the shooting died away.

CHAPTER IV

Y

AFTER TAKING OUR LESSONS TO HEART AND PILING INTO BED, we were awakened at 11:30 P.M. by a tremendous bombardment from big Jap naval guns. It seemed as if all the props had been kicked from under the sky and we were crushed beneath.

The thing started so suddenly we almost broke our necks getting into foxholes—and what foxholes! There had been no good tough shelling lately, and because of hot weather nobody had been inclined to do much digging. Duke Davis and I shared a hole six feet long and about eighteen inches deep. Lying side by side, squeezed together, we were pretty much exposed.

The ground was shaking and pitching from the violent concussions. We were shaking too—I'll admit that. We just about beat each other to death that night.

Jap planes overhead were dropping occasional white parachute flares and bombs. Fires set by the shelling lighted our area like day. A hundred yards away captured Jap gaso-

37

line in drums blazed with periodic explosions that shook
our back teeth.

Shell fragments, slashing overhead after each burst,
knocked down tents a few feet away, and the hot, jagged
pieces cut off dozens of palm trees.   .

Captain Gregory K. (Little Nemo) Loesch, twenty-three,
Montrose, Colorado, ran out of his tent a bit late and could
find no foxhole. "Hey, fellows!" he yelled, "have you got any
room over there?" Thinking he had asked for "rum," Haberman sang out, "No, but there's some in the tent!" Loesch
finally took refuge behind a fallen tree.

When there was a lull in the shelling, I crawled out of the
hole. Suddenly I heard more big ones coming. I returned to
the foxhole in a flying dive that just about killed Duke.

As we lay there, crowded and covered with dust, I absently
started beating a tune on Duke's helmet. Finally he could
stand it no longer. He yelled, "For God's sake, stop that. It
makes me nervous!"

The worst of the shelling was in the two hours between
one and three o'clock. Jap cruisers and destroyers were
parading up and down the channel, throwing everything
they had at us. Farther out to sea, an enemy battleship was
working us over with fourteen-inch shells. Overhead, circling
enemy planes dosed us with large bombs and small anti-
personnel bombs.

At the height of the bombardment the express train roar
of the bursting salvos was so loud that it overloaded the
capacity of the human ear. Those two hours were simply
indescribable. Nothing like them can be imagined.

Things quieted down after three o'clock, but the Japs
made sleep impossible by nuisance bombing raids which

continued till daylight. A series of air alerts began before breakfast. We walked around groggily picking up the pieces and viewing damage. A number of officers and men had been killed. One of them was Captain Ed Miller, my instructor when I was a cadet at Pensacola. He was a great guy and we all missed him.

Several of our planes were wrecked, and we found many deep craters in the field. These were repaired in short order. We picked up the heads from some fourteen-inchers and hung them up for gas alarm gongs.

At the edge of the field we saw several of the island's harsh-voiced, but beautiful parrots sitting on the ground, stunned by the explosions. Old-timers—the boys who had seen more than one war—said the night was the worst they had ever heard of.

Lieutenant Simpson, the Chicagoan, was the maddest man you ever saw. He had hung up his laundry the night before, and a jagged hunk of shell casing had gone right down the line, cutting hell out of everything.

Early that morning the dirt started to fly. Men were digging deeper foxholes everywhere. Nobody was going to be caught unprepared again.

Periodically Zeros broke loose from dogfights overhead and tried to strafe the field. Within a few hours the boys were up after a wave of bombers and had shot down a dozen.

At midmorning we went up to intercept a mass bombing attack. Dropping out of my flight due to a missing motor, I hid in clouds over the mountains because twenty-five high-flying bombers were loosing their cargoes on the field, and I could not come in. I looked up and saw a Grumman diving right in front of me with a Zero hot on his tail. The Grumman dove into a cloud and the Zero swung directly in front of me unknowingly. All I had to do was kick the plane around a little, and he was full in the sights. My touch on the trigger was as delicate as a drug-store clerk packing a pint of ice cream. The Jap's wing blew off, and he whirled into a cloud and disappeared. Afterward I saw the plane burning on the side of a mountain. It was Zero number two for me. I never got one any easier.

You might like to know how some of our combat victories were confirmed. Other flyers and observers on the ground with field glasses confirmed many. If a pilot happened to be alone and caused an enemy plane to explode or crash, he was entitled to claim it. But we were seldom alone. Lone Rangers made few successful rides in the sky over the Solomons. They had a habit of not coming back. The Japs were too alert for stragglers.

"Smokers"—enemy planes which disappeared in the distance, streaming smoke—were not counted, though they could not possibly have reached their base on Bougainville Island. Dark smoke meant a hit on the oil line and a burned out motor almost immediately. Light-colored smoke was usually not smoke at all, but escaping gasoline. That meant a sudden landing too.

Smokers often got away in hot combats when we were outnumbered. When we hit a Zero and saw him start smoking, we knew he was out of action and turned to somebody more dangerous. Sometimes we would have a Zero smoking nicely, then see a flight mate in trouble. Instead of polishing off the cripple, we rushed to the rescue. We never thought about personal scores in dogfights—there was too much else to do. It was weeks after my twenty-sixth credited victory, as a matter of fact, before I knew Captain Eddie Rickenbacker had shot down the same number of enemy aircraft in the first World War.

Later that day I led a raid on six troop transports which the Japs were trying to sneak in north of Santa Ysabel, accompanied by warships. We went through heavy anti-aircraft fire to strafe the decks, which were packed with standing soldiers. It was a slaughter—the slugs from my .50-caliber guns must have killed scores. I wish some of the boys we lost at Pearl Harbor could have been there to see it.

One of our men failed to come back. He was Lieutenant Paul S. (King Kong) Rutledge, of Seattle, Washington, a city that gave us many fine flyers. He was a big, easygoing fellow. We never heard what happened to him.

Lieutenant Edward P. (Andy) Andrews, a happy-go-lucky little daredevil from Liberty, Nebraska, went back alone and strafed all six transports again. He went right straight down the line, raked the deck of one ship, dropped over the stern, flying between that ship and the next so the two would not dare fire at him for fear of hitting each other, then raised up and dropped down on the next. He did this on all six. The convoy destroyers on each side did not dare shoot for fear of hitting their own ships. Our attacks badly damaged at least one transport. It was later found beached. For their part that day the Japs succeeded in setting fire to one of our cargo ships.

Japanese land batteries again shelled the airfield. A major land battle was obviously shaping in the jungle west of us. The Marines were reinforced now by Army troops under the command of Major General Millard F. Harmon of the air forces. It was plain that the Japs were assembling their forces for a heavy blow at the field. This was the very core of their strategy from the beginning—to recapture the field or, failing that, to reduce it to a condition useless for our purposes. Possession of that little cleared stretch was the only thing that enabled our out-numbered forces to hold out on Guadalcanal at that stage.

At 2 A.M. Jap warships gave us a light going over, but their enthusiasm of the night before was lacking. No fourteen-inch shells landed. We heard later that one of our bombers had laid a five-hundred-pound egg on a Jap battle wagon far offshore—which no doubt explained the big boy's failure to take part in the nocturnal festivities. The Japs were successful that night, however, in landing heavy reinforcements. The estimates ran as high as 20,000 troops. Heavy artillery and tanks were also unloaded—a poor omen for the future.

Five Zeros flew high over Henderson Field early in the morning and scribbled a broken circle of smoke across our positions—apparently to guide following waves of bombers. Soon twenty-eight high altitude bombers appeared, and we were on our way up after them. I remember slashing in to attack. There were Zeros and bombers on both sides, and I was twisting my head watchfully. The next thing I knew I was below a thousand feet and saw mountains on my left.

It was a narrow escape. Looking around, I had twisted my oxygen mask loose and lost consciousness without going through any stage of discomfort whatever. Occasionally we lost a man like that. The masks were pretty good ones but not entirely proof against carelessness.

Full of fear, my wingman, Captain Loesch, followed me

down on that dive, and said I wheeled her out just before he gave up all hope. I landed after that.

When the boys returned, we went out to strafe transports and cargo ships which were unloading supplies between Henderson Field and Cape Esperance, about ten miles northwest of Lunga point. That these ships were there at all was due to the fact that we were short of gasoline and couldn't keep up continuous aerial attacks. They were the five ships which had survived our attentions of the day before. Protected by eight destroyers, they were discovered at dawn, and our bombers began working on them without delay.

We strafed the decks as well as cutting up ground installations on the beach. Our dive bombers came over the hills, peeled off, and attacked from the northwest. They set one ship on fire, then a second, despite heavy anti-aircraft fire. Flame and black smoke came up in great bursts.

Meanwhile Major Cram, aide to General Geiger, loaded two torpedoes into the general's personal PBY. He had never dropped a torpedo before. Someone told him how to do it, and a couple of minutes later he was off, flying without a co-pilot.

He circled inside the bombers near the beach west of Kokumbona, taking advantage of every bit of cloud cover, then attacked from the opposite direction. He was able to get in close before the destroyers saw him. They sent him everything they had, but he got down close to the water and came in, disregarding the fire. He lined up the transports and let go his first torpedo at about five hundred yards. Then he lined up the others and sent the second torpedo away. One of them got a solid hit. The transport blew up and sank within a few minutes.

The Major made a quick flipper turn to the left and again ran the gauntlet of AA fire on his way back to the field, eight miles away. At that point the Japs gave up unloading operations for the day. Destroyers closed their aprons around the two remaining ships and ushered them out to sea again.

While Major Cram was pressing home his attack, Zeros were after him, and they followed him back to the field. We attacked the Zeros and shot down several.

Although his plane had been shot up and was squirting oil like a fire hose, old Rog Haberman was in that fight. He didn't get anything his first run but came around again and knifed up to within forty feet of the remaining Zero that was working on the PBY.

The Major had swung over the field by that time. Haberman could have read a postcard over the Jap's shoulder when he finally cut loose. The Zero disintegrated with a flash, completely hiding the Grumman from sight. Pieces burned just off the field, to the huge delight of the ground forces. With a smoking plane, Haberman did a quick wingover and landed on the field. He was yelling his head off— it was his first Zero.

He helped the Major and his crew out of a hot spot on that deal. Not only that, the "Old Man" might have been peeved if his plane hadn't come back.

General Geiger was stocky, witty, and tough—a true Marine. He was fifty-seven years old. His headquarters was dug into the slope of a hill a quarter of a mile from the fighter ready-tent area, and was vulnerable to shell and bomb hits.

I don't believe he ever gave a thought to his personal safety. Once, just for fun, he loaded a thousand-pound egg onto a dive bomber and went up over the hills to bomb the Japs on a ridge. He got a good hit, too.

He often sat at fighter headquarters, watching patrols take off. One dawn an unlucky pilot, with his eyes still blurry from sleep, taxied into a bomb crater and wrecked his prop. I sent for him. When the young lieutenant came up, the General glowered at him and snapped, "Was that necessary?" It was all he said, but it was enough.

Old friends called him "Jiggs," but I never did, not wanting to be working for nothing.

He got a great kick out of his membership in the Short Snorters. To be eligible for this outfit you are supposed to have flown over a thousand miles of water, shot a moose, or slept with an Eskimo. The boys trade signatures on paper currency, and if anyone is caught with his "membership card" more than two minutes away, he must pay a dollar to everybody in the crowd.

It tickled the General to find someone without his "card." Major Cram, who believed in physical fitness, took a two-mile run every day in his shorts. Once the General watched till Jack got too far away to sprint back in two minutes. Then he hopped into a jeep, caught Jack, and demanded proof of membership. The Major paid.

Lieutenant E. T. (Smokey) Stover, twenty-two, of Eureka Springs, Arkansas, a dark, chunky naval flyer from Fighting 5 squadron, celebrated the squadron's last day on the island by bringing back part of a Zero's wing insignia, ripped off in a mid-air collision.

Smokey was one of the many pilots occupied in strafing the transports off Cape Esperance. After he had made two runs, a Jap biplane came along—one of the newer cruiser planes with a rear gunner. Smokey made a head-on run, firing all six guns. The Jap showed no evidence of being hit. As Smokey pulled up to avoid a collision, he miscalculated a little and the two planes brushed together. The biplane wobbled, went out of control, spun down, and crashed in the mountains.

Mechanics found a big hole in Smokey's right wing when he landed. Also caught on the wing was a yard-square strip of black fabric containing part of a blood-red Rising Sun, edged with a gray circle.

Fighting 5 had a score of ninety-eight Jap planes when it left Guadalcanal.

CHAPTER V

Y

WE HAD AN OLD "TARP" STRETCHED OVER THE TOPS OF LARGE poles to roof our dining hall. By "we" I mean, of course, us and the flies. We slept from two to six in a tent. Some of us always were out before dawn, ready for surprise attacks. Drinking cocoa, we watched "mechs" start the planes, check magnetos, props, engine, and tabs. Ordnance men checked the guns and saw that ammunition pans were full.

Breakfast came along about 8 A.M. It might be pancakes and hash, with coffee. Or cereal—dehydrated eggs and bacon once in a while. That was all right with me—about the eggs, I mean. They were pretty sad. They stunk so we had to avert our faces when we ate them. When I got back to the States, I was introduced to a fellow who said he ran one of the dehydrating plants. I told him what I thought of his product in a few short words. He apologized and said the process had been much improved. I was glad to hear that.

After breakfast there was the endless vigil of the ready tent, where some of the boys lay comfortably on cots and

47

others just sat on the backs of their necks. A phonograph blared out some old tune. Sometimes there were fairly recent (only a few months old) magazines or newspapers to read. We played checkers, cribbage, or acey-deucy, a two-man game managed with dice. Sometimes we just sat and shot the breeze, talking about things back home, or discussed tactics by the hour. Often we'd sleep in the daytime, since the Japs kept us awake so much at night.

Occasionally there was a scramble, or maybe we were alerted by a bogey—a report of unidentified approaching aircraft. "A formation of parrots" was another term we had for these bogeys. For lunch at noon there was invariably soup or stew, with crackers. Supper was at four. We would have Spam and Spam or Vienna sausage and more Spam, or perhaps vice versa for a change. With it there would be de-hydrated potatoes, the most successful of all these dried foods; vegetables, and canned peaches. Afterward two eight-man flights remained on duty until dark. The other men were free, which meant usually a shower at the power plant on the Lunga River, where warm water ran out. The shower was something to look forward to all day.

Out in the bright sun we wore baseball caps—blue for pilots and red for mechanics—to protect our eyes. I had something better than baseball headgear—an old canvas hunting cap that I've worn for eight or ten years. It is faded almost white but is still serviceable. Shaving was optional, and most of us took a crack at growing a beard. Clothing was Marine issue shoes, socks, "skivvy" shirts and drawers, khaki shirts and pants, summer flying suits or coveralls. Each man wore a .45 caliber pistol and a knife with six-inch blade. The knife was in case of jungle landings.

These are two of Joe's friends: Major Leonard (Duke) Davis, left, squadron commander, and Sergeant Joe Palko, right, of Hazelton, Pa., "The Fighting Hunky," later killed in action.

Staff Sergeant James Feliton, of Syracuse, N. Y., with natives who brought him back after he had been forced to parachute thirty miles behind the lines. The natives are holding gifts.

Joe Foss, at that time a captain, is shown here on Guadalcanal with Major General Roy S. Geiger, director of Marine Corps Aviation, discussing the aerial tactics which routed the Japs.

(Official U. S. Marine Corps Photo)

By the end of our first week on Guadalcanal even the most excitement-crazy could see that they had arrived in time for the big stuff after all. The air was filled with danger. Night and day bombing attacks, shelling from the jungle and the sea, the spatter of snipers' bullets—all these were our steady diet.

Nuisance night raids were a cunning device to rob us of sleep, and made a liar out of the gent who spoke of the Japanese sandman bringing sweet dreams. On the night of October 16, for example, a crazy Jap swept so low over the field that his rear gunner was able to strafe with a machine gun, doing little damage but being a great bother so far as sleep was concerned.

His plane sounded just like a popcorn machine. While this boob was flying around shooting, everybody ran out of the tents and cut loose at him with pistols or anything. It was the funniest thing I ever heard of in my life—this Jap plane flying around in the dark all alone and everybody shooting at it. I was in the sack when it started, but got out of there in short order.

A little later two more planes came over and dropped bombs. One five-hundred-pounder landed about ten feet ahead of my plane but did little damage except for one queer thing. A flying fragment cut off my throttle handle.

For the third straight night we were bombarded by warships, which poured hundreds of shells into our area. The attack started a few minutes after midnight, and the Japs did a leisurely job of it as they hammered the field and shore installations. Some of the boys counted 130 shells within fifteen minutes.

I took off on a morning mission to strafe the valley in

which the Japs had been concentrating supplies west of Henderson Field. We flew within a few feet of the treetops so the anti-aircraft was unable to get any bead on us. Our dive bombers spotted and destroyed several AA positions with the loss of only one plane.

After returning to the field to regas and reload, we strafed landing barges all along the beach so they could not be used again. Wherever our .50 caliber bullets hit, they punched big holes. When they happened to hit a Jap, they almost literally turned him wrong side out—and I'm not kidding.

We were extremely low on gasoline and resorted to all means of getting it, including the draining of wrecked airplanes. After evening chow, all the flyers were happy because a gas barge was pulling in, and a veteran squadron led by Lieutenant Colonel Harold W. (Joe) Bauer, of Coronado, California, our fighter commander, was coming in to help us.

The Colonel's squadron had flown from another island as evening was approaching, and his boys were landing when a thing happened that plunged us into bitter gloom.

Most of the planes were on the ground already when Jap dive bombers were sighted in full dive, coming down to hit the gas barge.

The third plane down made a direct hit—which was the end of the barge. Then the remainder of the bombers came on in.

Colonel Bauer was so incensed he raced after them alone and shot down four in quick succession, almost as quickly as you read these words. This feat was accomplished in full view of all of us on the field, and at an altitude of only a few hundred feet.

Our precious gasoline was lost, but the quick avenging

guns of Colonel Bauer made us feel a little better. He was such a dynamic leader that when he landed and gave us a short pep talk, we got our chins off our chests and were ready to go again.

Hundreds of Marines swimming in the Lunga River or gathered along the banks washing clothes were scattered by the unexpected attack. Three sailors were killed. The heroism of coxswain "Shanghai" Rheindt and shipfitter Edward E. Witt saved many other lives, however. They drove their boat through flaming gasoline to pick up survivors.

Our bombers came back from a raid on the Jap base at Rekata Bay, on the northwest shore of Santa Ysabel Island, 135 miles away. They had set fuel storage facilities afire, put anti-aircraft batteries out of commission, and destroyed fourteen enemy planes, twelve of them on the ground. Four direct bomb hits that day completed destruction of two out of three beached transports on the northwest coast of Guadalcanal.

Our gasoline situation—which the enemy fortunately didn't know about—made this period the blackest in the aerial history of that campaign, but the boys weren't licked. Next morning the flight led by Duke went up over Tulagi and knocked down an entire group of eight dive bombers and four out of eight Zeros within a few minutes. I slept late but was awakened by the dogfights and emerged in time to watch Jap planes falling—a sight none of us ever tired of. One stricken bomber dropped its load into the sea near Tulagi, raising tall columns of water. At the same time the crippled plane floated down out of the sky like a burning bit of paper. Another angled gracefully into the sea, trailing smoke. It burst into flames after smacking the water nose first, and its death was quickly hidden behind a thick screen of black smoke. One of our pilots didn't come back from that fight.

Meanwhile, six other bombers attacked two American destroyers in the channel. Anti-aircraft gunners picked them off one by one before they could do any damage. The best the Japs could do was a near miss.

One Zero pilot, a good man, too, got on the tail of a Wildcat over Henderson Field and for a time it looked like curtains for the Grumman. The planes streaked through the sky, diving, turning, and twisting, but our man couldn't shake the Jap. Finally he pulled out suddenly from a long swoop, and the Zero overran, disappearing behind a hill as he pulled out.

In a moment he was back, climbing like an elevator as AA fire boxed him in. He managed to escape, but a few seconds later a couple of machine gunners on the beach brought him down flaming. It was the three hundred and seventh Jap plane shot down in the small Solomon Islands theater since August 7.

Right after that our destroyers in the channel began making leisurely runs, pouring shells into the Jap shore positions west of the field. In three hours and twenty minutes they made six runs, firing 1,900 rounds by actual count. The shells started many small fires near the Jap landing boats and huts. Three fires were big enough to be visible for fifteen miles. One covered an area about three hundred yards square.

The enemy retaliated by sending over sixteen bombers with fighter escort in a high level attack on the field. None of the bombers was shot down, but one was smoking as they pulled away.

Coming down fast in a power dive, some of our pilots hemorrhaged their eardrums. One of them was Lieutenant Jack E. Conger, twenty-one, of Des Moines, Iowa. Jack had come in the night before with Colonel Bauer's outfit, which had been away for a rest since October 2. He felt a terrific pain in his ears as he was coming down. Suddenly it stopped. On the ground a doctor looked down his throat and told him it was a hemorrhage but not anything serious. This happens to a good many pilots at one time or another. On the same hop, Jack's flight mate, Lieutenant Forbes (Blackie) Bastian, twenty-one, a New Orleans boy, broke one eardrum and hemorrhaged the other.

My job came later when I took a late evening patrol to strafe hell out of the Jap camps. No shells were fired at us as we came in for a surprise attack over the mountains.

The evening was a fine one for love or sleep, as the moon was out and a cool breeze was blowing. However, we enjoyed neither recreation. Jap warships and land batteries shelled us again, and our guns answered, all adding up to not much sleep.

We took to the foxholes. We had deeper and better foxholes by this time. We had foxholes with tops on them so thick it would take direct hits to unearth us. We had steel plates on top of them and logs and dirt and sandbags on top of that. These holes smelled like an owl's nest. They were damp and moldy, and when it rained, we were bogged in mud. They never dried out.

But they were a comfort. Once a shell landed close enough to our bivouac area to throw dirt on the table. Every time we heard the whistle of an approaching shell, we dropped to the ground. An argument started as to whether or not it was too late to drop after we heard the whistle, but I noticed the man who argued it was too late was always the first one down.

The enemy was getting better prepared for his big push. We were trying desperately to keep him off balance until our side could bring up more power. Big bombers commanded by Brigadier General Laverne Saunders, of Aberdeen, South Dakota, an SAE brother of mine from the Vermillion chapter, helped rock the Jap back on his heels in those days when we were fighting for time. The Navy was a major help. Again on the eighteenth destroyers bombarded enemy installations and blew up munitions dumps. Colonel Bauer issued this order: "When you see Zeros, dogfight 'em!"

An unexplainable tragedy marred our next take-off. As we went up on an interception, Lieutenant Andy Andrews, the little powerhouse from Nebraska, lost control of his Wildcat, crashed into a parked plane, and was killed. I don't need to tell you how we felt at a time like that. Maybe it was a good thing we had to keep right on going up to attack.

Due to the accident, two of the boys—Bill Marontate and Danny Doyle—were delayed in taking off and were a little behind the other five of us. We turned and kept scissoring (circling and turning in toward each other) back and forth while waiting for them to join us.

Marontate and Doyle were a couple of thousand feet below. On one turn I noticed there were five planes below—not two. On closer view I could see three of them were Zeros. They were flying a few feet behind the Marines with the apparent idea of knocking off those two planes and then any others they could surprise.

We slid gently down behind them and started shooting. I picked the Zero farthest to the left. My first tracers set him afire, and he tipped over into a spin and went in.

Marontate and Doyle didn't know they were in danger till our tracers went by their ears. They turned, but already the rest of us had polished off the three Zeros.

Then came other Zeros from above, precipitating a general dogfight. The prospective victim I selected was tough—I couldn't get behind him. I shot at him from the side, and the bullets looked as if they were going into the cockpit. But apparently they went in back of the motor somewhere, for he started smoking. Whether he went down or not I do not know, because I jumped immediately into action with another Zero.

The second time we approached head on, I held my fire until he was close in, and he pulled up. As he did so, I had barely shot at him when he burst into flames. He did a tight wingover, blazing fiercely, and I pulled off and saw him far below, going down in flames. There were other Zeros, too, down there smoking.

I looked off in the distance and saw the bombers we were expecting. They were what we called Type I—twin-motored jobs resembling our B-25s somewhat. I climbed to meet them on a 180° course and made a run on the right rear bomber —the one on the right echelon. As I came down in a vertical dive, making my run and ready to shoot, he suddenly blew up. One of his tanks had exploded, though I hadn't fired a single shot. I later found out it was Ensign "Red" Thrash, a Navy pilot, who got him.

I pulled through the pieces, moved up and shot at the next bomber in the echelon. By that time I was too close for anything but a short burst, which started smoke but produced no fire or explosion.

Then I dove and came up under the left wing of the V formation, taking a belly shot at the last plane in line. It was a direct hit which caused an explosion and fire on the left motor. I was right under him, my nose pointing straight up, and the plane almost in a complete stall. It was impossible to miss. It was like pointing a pistol straight up in a room—you cannot help hitting the ceiling.

He went down at a 45° angle. Bombers all go down the same way when you get them. There's a big burst of fire, which dies down, goes "whooooosh!" again, dies down, and repeats. Pretty soon a wing drops off and the bomber goes into a final spin.

This one struck the water between Henderson Field and Tulagi, right in the middle of the channel. It went right on in full tilt but three Japs out of the crew of six or seven lived. They didn't even have a scratch on them—nobody could figure it out.

I returned to the field, ammunition gone, with Zeros in hot pursuit. I landed out of gas.

Men from VMF 212 also took part in that fight and deserve their share of the credit. Captain D. R. (Doc) Everton, a Crofton, Nebraska, pilot so nicknamed because he once studied medicine, led Conger, Bastian, and Gunner "Tex" Hamilton, a Texan who held the rank of warrant officer, into the melee. When Zeros swooped, Captain Everton blocked them out. Conger made his run on a bomber, firing. Nothing happened. When he was within two hundred feet, the entire left side of the bomber exploded and flamed. The heat was so intense Jack felt it in his cockpit as he swerved. Bastian, coming behind, was caught in the actual flames and momentarily couldn't figure out where he was.

Before he knew how he'd done it, Conger found himself on the tail of a Zero. As he fired, it blazed where the wings fasten to the fuselage, and spiraled to a crash far below.

Lieutenant "Father" Flaherty, from Waterloo, Iowa, was missing from 212 when it was all over. Someone said they saw him pounded into the sea by two Zeros.

That flight cost us. Andrews had been killed at the take-off, and Lieutenant Lowell D. Grow, twenty-two, of Huntsville, Utah, a quiet fellow who always carried out his orders without comment, did not return. But we did pretty well for youngsters, knocking down eight bombers and eleven Zeros out of a flight of twenty bombers and twenty Zeros, with the loss of only three men.

CHAPTER VI

Υ

WE TOOK THE NEXT DAY OFF AND HIKED UP TO THE FRONT LINES for a look around. I swapped stories with the ground boys and gave them some candy I had. Then I returned to do my washing in the river. There was a large tree that had fallen across the stream, and we used it for a washboard to scrub our clothes on, standing in the river and working industriously. The water was swift, cold, and full of silt.

I couldn't get my things clean, so I took them back to camp and put them in a can of water, lighted a fire under the can, and boiled them. Not thinking about a pair of cheap colored socks, I boiled these with the shirts and underwear. The result was wine red shirts and underwear—and I do mean red.

In a dogfight, Lieutenant Clair Chamberlain, Rochester, Minnesota, got five pieces of shrapnel from a 20-mm. cannon in his shoulder blade and was hospitalized. Next day another man from 212—Captain Everton—was shot in the right thigh and laid up after bagging two Zeros.

58

This ended a little time of comparative peace before the storm that we knew must break soon. At 10:15 A.M. on the twentieth, after a blessedly quiet night, our flight took off to intercept eighteen Zeros. On the first head-on attack a Zero drove straight at me, high over the water between Henderson Field and little Savo Island.

I had not started shooting yet, but already his bullets were streaming beneath me. Then, as he pulled up to correct his aim, his bullets continued to miss, although they came within a few inches of my wing tips.

We were close together now, and I could see the hot tracers swishing past as he decided to turn out. When he maneuvered, I bore around hard, swung onto his tail, and put a long burst into his wing base.

His plane blew up with a bright flash and a shattering roar, high up there in the sky. Big pieces went hurtling down to the water, far below, while the little pieces followed leisurely.

In an instant I was engaged with another Zero. We both tried to make long runs at each other, but neither seemed able to get a decent shot.

Finally I did a quick wingover, came down and made a deflected (side) shot at extremely close range. This was an odd thing. My bullets hit the side of the cockpit. The plane went into a spin with no signs of smoke or fire, and continued to spin down with increasing momentum.

I watched it twist downward for thousands of feet—on into the channel, where its impact raised a towering plume of water. The pilot never showed any signs of life or attempted to pull out. Apparently I had killed him.

We seldom had time, up there in that unhealthy sky, to

watch our victims fall. It was a little different today, because right after I had delivered my burst a Zero came by and gave me a dose of bullets which caused my motor to start smoking and burn out. I went into a long glide for the field, making it without any trouble. Those two Zeros brought my score to seven.

One of my flight—Lieutenant Eugene A. (Gene) Nuwer, of Lancaster, New York, failed to return from that hop. The last I saw of him he was in full dive on the tail of a Zero with another Zero on his tail. What happened to him I never learned.

Our next action developed when dive bombers were spotted coming in for an attack on the field the following day. All our fighters were at high altitude engaging Zeros and did not see the bombers. I got permission from Colonel Bauer to take off in the one Wildcat remaining on the field. I hoped to catch them as they came out of the dive.

That plane had been grounded, but no one seemed to know why. After checking the motor—it seemed to run all right—I attempted to take off. Things did not sound too good then, so I cut the throttle and taxied back to try a second time.

On this attempt the plane got about twenty feet in the air before the motor cut out completely at the end of the field, right over innumerable palm tree stumps. That was a poor place to be without power. My landing gear struck a stump and ripped off. I hit a second stump with terrific force, and the plane stopped cold. I kept on going till my head struck something which raised a big bump and tore a gouge out of my helmet.

I jumped out of the plane hurriedly, afraid of fire, and,

since there was nothing better to do at the moment, walked over and sat down in the shade of a tree. There was a minor cut on my head which was beginning to bleed.

An ambulance came tearing up with a doctor in it, my old friend of the ocean voyage, Doc Peterson. He took a quick look in the plane, then around it, and couldn't find me. I yelled, "Hey, Doc, here I am." By this time the cut on my head was bleeding freely, sending streams down the side of my face. I guess I looked like a real case for the hospital. But I was really all right.

Five fellows from 212 were tangled with eight Zeros in a fierce dogfight but came out well. Conger, a little fellow, full of mustard, who once lived in my home town, got one Zero. Major Frederick Payne, a thirty-one-year-old Californian who was executive officer of the squadron, got one. Lieutenant Frank Drury, twenty-two, of Danby, Missouri, got two and Blackie Bastian one. That wasn't all Bastian got. He was shot in the neck—put out of action with a crease one's finger could be laid in. But he managed to land all right. Later Blackie swore he saw the Jap bullet coming straight for his head and almost succeeded in ducking it.

Tex Hamilton didn't come back. Drury told of seeing a flyer in a yellow life jacket descending in a chute. Japs use white life jackets. Drury flew around the falling man, who hung limp in his chute. We never heard anything more of him. Tex was a handy veteran who had been flying since 1936 and made more money than the young lieutenants, in spite of his rank.

Six bombers and six fighters was the day's score. Antiaircraft destroyed one bomber and got pieces of two others.

I wound up the day flying night patrol, looking for "Maytag Charlie." That was the name we had for a Jap who flew over nearly every night in some kind of a seaplane that sounded like a washing machine. Sometimes he dropped a bomb; sometimes he didn't. But he never showed up that time.

Other late Jap flyers, however, dished up a thirty-one bomb salute for the arrival of the Number One Marine, Lieutenant General Thomas Holcomb, commandant of the corps. He arrived at dusk with a heavy fighter escort just as the Japs were giving us the usual high altitude nuisance bombing. In his party were Major General Ralph Mitchell, head of Marine aviation, and Brigadier General Bennett Puryear, Jr., Marine quartermaster, in charge of the handling of supplies.

During his short stay on the island General Holcomb visited all the air units as well as every battalion on the firing line. At noon on the next day, despite bad flying weather, my boys gave him a demonstration by shooting down every plane in a group of five dive bombers which came over. None of our planes was touched. I had to return to the field because of oxygen trouble and didn't get in on the fun. This was the seventy-ninth Jap raid in little more than two months. The day's results brought enemy planes shot down in actual air combat to 290 as against 62 of ours—not quite five to one.

Touring the island with General Vandegrift and other officers, General Holcomb went into the jungle in a procession of jeeps, pushing aside vines and creepers hanging from the great banyan trees. He visited the front lines on foot and wound up by crossing a stream in a rubber boat. At mealtimes he got samples of the work of "Millimeter Pete," the Jap artilleryman who always shelled the field just when we had tucked our feet under the table.

I took the evening patrol and strafed the Jap lines. There was no sign of enemy fire.

October 23 opened as a dull day, despite the certainty that the Japs were ready to begin their big drive at any hour. The rainy season was starting. Early in the morning we escorted General Holcomb, General Mitchell, and the others down the channel. They were in a PBY, bound perhaps for New Caledonia, though we didn't ask.

We made that flight with a little reluctance, for we feared not being included in the day's other hops, because of already having had our turn. After the mission was over, we lounged around all morning—then got welcome orders to scramble at noon. •

High in the sunny sky were sixteen silver bombers, on their way to bomb the harbor shipping. My flight and several others took off with a snap.

Off to the side we spotted five Zeros—two in one group and three in the other. They must have seen us at the same time, because they swung around in a big arc to get on our tails. My flight was in the rear, and I swung around to meet them. The other flight, commanded by Major Davis, turned too.

As we started to close in, I took a good look around. Looking doesn't cost anything and is a healthy habit for pilots to develop. It was especially healthy here, for high above, like the painting of a flight of birds, eighteen to twenty Zeros were in full, screaming dive.

I tell you we made a quick turn and got into a dive ourselves to get up momentum. With the speed of thought,

Duke's flight was engaged. Planes were starting to fall. Duke's boys were knocking them down already.

The first thing I knew a Grumman came across my course at an angle, pouring lead into a Zero that was trying to get away. On the Wildcat's tail another Zero was hanging, pumping away with machine guns and cannon.

I swung in behind this Zero. When I was only a few feet away, I gave it to him. Poof! He blew up and disintegrated.

No words can overpicture the explosion of a Zero, or exaggerate the thrill it gives you. The motor goes off in a crazy, lopsided whirl. The pilot pops out of his cockpit like a pea that has been pressed from the pod. The air is filled with dust and little pieces, as if someone had emptied a huge vacuum cleaner bag in the sky. The wing section, burning where it had joined the fuselage, takes a long time to fall. It goes down like a leaf—sailing, then almost stopping as it attacks the air, sailing again, and attacking the air again.

I swung over hard to miss the falling junk. The sky was filled with wild dogfights. I got onto the tail of a Jap, but he saw me coming and went into a dive. Then he pulled out and went into a loop. I cut close inside and as he went over on his back, I thought, hell, this is the thing I've been waiting for. I was upside down when I led him with a good spray from my six .50-caliber machine guns. The fire converged into a lucky shot. He blew up in a great, beautiful burst, and I ducked as the Grumman went through the pieces.

I was conscious of explosions, fires, and streams of tracers on all sides. The dogfight was wound up tight in a small area, and the sky was filled with death. I came out of the loop and put my nose down to gain speed.

Out of nowhere came a maniac in a Zero, going up at an angle and breaking into a slow roll. He must have thought he got somebody and was due for a celebration. When he was three-quarters around, I pulled up and gave him a quick squirt. There was a lovely, blinding flash, and the pilot popped out, nearly hitting my Grumman. I barely managed to hop over him as he plummeted down toward the island and the sea, both looking so incredibly peaceful below.

But this was no spot for a nature lover. Leveling out of a dive, two Zeros were coming for me—one head on, the other from an angle. I made for the first one. While I was wondering if he intended to ram me, he pulled up to his right. I got in a short burst back of his motor, and flames were lapping at him as I went on by. He blew up when right off my left wing.

While this was happening, another Zero must have climbed onto my tail, because tracers were going by. Something had gone wrong with my motor too. This lad who had come in with the head on attack must have hit me. I remembered he had been doing a lot of shooting, and at that range it would be hard to miss. The motor began to smoke.

I pushed over to pick up speed and thanked the Lord for plenty of altitude. With increasing momentum I was smoking like a skywriter. The Jap behind dove after me, overran, then pulled up and made a spiral turn. I got in a short burst with no apparent effect and then ran out of ammunition.

Another Zero wheeled by and sprinkled me good and plenty before turning off on the heels of the other. I suddenly yearned to be somewhere else. It is no fun playing with these boys when you do not even have a bean in your guns. By radio, I called for reinforcements. Two of our men, having the situation exceedingly well in hand by then, came over. I am happy to say they polished off both Zeros, though I did not see the fight.

At that time I was busy worrying about getting home to Henderson Field. It was a long glide from altitude, and I had plenty of time to think.

Here it was the twenty-third of October, and we had been on the island about two weeks. My lucky streak that day brought my bag of enemy planes to eleven—a respectable number, but nothing extraordinary.

I thought affectionately of the good Grummans—they never blazed up. I only knew of one that ever did, and then it was a fluke. This had been a good day.

I reached the field all right. My oil line and wing tips had been hit. I was a little ashamed of myself.

"This," I thought, "is the fourth Grumman I've brought down in bad shape. Just one more and I'll be a Japanese ace!"

Overhead, meanwhile, one of the best dogfights of all time was about over. Columns of smoke were visible at sea and on the island where blazing Zeros had plunged. A flaming Zero streaked toward the water, with a blazing parachute following behind. Half a mile away another Zero spiraled down, while its pilot stood almost motionless in the sky, supported by his parachute. Later he came down in the sea, and our boats sped out to pick him up.

A last remaining Zero tangled with three Grummans high above. Climbing vertically, he started smoking, slowed, nosed over, and began to fall, smoking more noticeably. Suddenly he was ripped apart by a monstrous explosion. The big pieces, flaming, fell in a vertical dive which left a tall feather of smoke laid against the sky.

The boys started coming in, some smoking, all filled with tales of their exploits. One Grumman was so full of holes it was pushed off to the boneyard without further ado. Little Jack Conger got a Zero in a particularly satisfying manner. He selected his victim, put in a good burst and saw a big puff of white smoke—probably gasoline spray. The Zero headed back toward Bougainville, losing altitude. Conger pursued vengefully. Over Savo he was a bare hundred feet behind. Aiming carefully, he sent home a great burst of .50-caliber slugs. The Zero exploded so violently the pilot was blown from his cockpit. His chute, riddled, flopped like a wet sack as he fell.

All squadrons combined got twenty Zeros and a bomber that day. And Father Flaherty returned in triumph. He was found on Savo Island, where natives were giving him a royal feast.

We weren't always so lucky, but it did happen that day that all of our boys returned.

CHAPTER VII

Y

THE RAINS CAME, AND THE JAPS AT LAST BEGAN THEIR GREAT full-scale offensive off in the jungle. But they got it off without aerial support. The twenty-third seemed to be all their flyers wanted for a while. After a night in which the constant roar of land artillery lulled us to sleep, we put in a quiet day as far as flying went. No combat. No Japs came. It had rained several inches during the night, and the downpour continued. Shells also rained without interruption from the artillery of both sides.

We learned that the Japanese land attack—made after dark, as usual—was led by a dozen small tanks. In a seven-hour battle along the mouth of the strategic Matanikau River, Marine troops smashed nine of the tanks and slaughtered six hundred Jap infantrymen. Aided by flares, some of our planes helped to repel the attack. One Jap tank, hit by grenades and artillery fire, whirled crazily out to sea, still firing in every direction. Next day it was found, turret deep in the water, swathed in our barbed wire and with two dead crewmen inside.

68

This fighting was within a half mile of our fighter strip, which made everything cozy. Next night they assaulted and dented the opposite end of our line, a mile south of the field and east of the Lunga River. Reinforcements were rushed up and saved the situation.

During the morning, dizzy from lack of sleep, I walked up and saw hundreds of dead Japs, in all the queer attitudes of death. They were stacked behind our lines, which by then were straightened. The little men had been brought down by artillery, mortar, and canister fire (scattering shot like ball bearings), machine guns, and rifles. On top of that, Army P-39s had strafed them from the air.

Sunday came—the Japs' favorite day for attack. Heavy rains had made our cow pasture field a quagmire, and we were helpless when waves of Zeros came over at 8 A.M. They circled at will, waiting to jump us when we took off.

Three Jap destroyers chose this time to sail boldly into the channel between Savo and Florida Islands, chasing two of our corvettes. The Japs had temporary control of the sea lanes at that time—a destroyer had penetrated close enough to Tulagi harbor a little earlier to sink the fleet tug *Seminole* and a harbor patrol boat. Our shore batteries got three hits on that destroyer, and planes went out to do some more damage.

On this morning the three Jap warships easily overran one corvette, sinking it and at the same time shelling our land batteries. The second corvette tried to escape but saw he couldn't make it. He turned gallantly, broke out his colors, and steamed straight for the Japs, firing his little three-inch gun in history's most unequal battle. He was blown out of the water, of course. All hands on both the little boats were later saved.

A few minutes later, at nine o'clock, we managed a take-off. I was the first one up, but others quickly followed. Most of us were immediately engaged by Zeros, but four men from another flight went out for revenge against the destroyers. One of them—Lieutenant "Cowboy" Stout, of Laramie, Wyoming—asked and received radio permission to strafe.

With Lieutenants Conger, Drury, and "Cloudy" Faulkner, of Pleasant Hill, Missouri, he methodically pumped .50-caliber fire into the water line of the destroyers for about four minutes while deck crews ran around like ants on a hot stove. Zeros then interrupted the game. Ammunition was running low anyway. Stout was actually out and needed an escort.

Faulkner, Drury, and Conger screened off the Zeros as Stout streaked in and landed safely. Faulkner and Drury each got a victim in the process. Conger sent in a short burst, saw the enemy smoking, but didn't see what happened after that.

He was too busy. Just off the beach at 1,500 feet he was attacked by another Zero. Both planes were firing when Conger ran out of ammunition. As the enemy passed overhead, Jack decided on a daring maneuver. Horsing back on the stick, he sent the Grumman's nose straight up. The engine and left wing hit the Zero, chewing off five feet of its tail—much more than he intended.

The Grumman went into a spin. Conger tried to right it, but the controls did not respond. He unhooked his safety

belt and was half out of the cockpit when the holster of his
.45 caught and refused to budge.

Finally he fought free and jumped. After the chute
popped, he swung only twice before hitting the water of
Guadalcanal Bay. He swam under water a little way, un-
snapped the chute, inflated his life jacket, and started swimming toward shore, half a mile distant.

A flaming Zero crashed into the water a hundred yards
to his left. A moment later, twenty yards ahead—between
Conger and the shore—a Jap pilot hit the water.

Conger stopped swimming and eyed the Jap. The Jap
stared back. A Higgins boat manned by sailors and Marines
broke the deadlock by picking Conger up.

There was an argument about the Jap. The Marines
wanted to take no chances. Jack wanted to bring in a prisoner. He finally out-yelled the Marines. But the Jap pushed
the boat away with his feet when it approached. Two more
boats came up and they surrounded him. Jack caught the
Jap's belt with a grappling hook and started to haul him
aboard.

The Jap rammed a pistol into Conger's face and pulled
the trigger. The gun clicked. Conger released the hook and
fell into the bottom of the boat. The Jap went back into the
water. He put the pistol to his head and pulled the trigger
again. There was the same waterlogged click.

A sailor grabbed the gun—a German Mauser—and they
finally hauled him aboard.

Afterward the Jap, who spoke English, would say only
that he once attended Tokyo University. He was not bad-
looking, but burned about the eyes. Conger got his flying

suit. The sailor kept the pistol—a souvenir Conger probably would have prized.

Ashore, three other flyers had seen Conger's "smoker" crash in flames. That gave him a score of two Zeros for the day. Colonel Bauer called him in.

"You fellows might be interested," he said, "in a call I just had from General Geiger. He congratulates the squadron on sinking two of the three Jap ships you strafed this morning. Our scouts report those destroyers sank immediately afterward. I'm giving you official credit for half a destroyer each."

Conger found it hard to believe that destroyers could be sunk by .50-caliber machine-gun bullets. But similar cases had been reported. "Anyway," he told Colonel Bauer, "you can't argue with a general."

We had barely reached 1,500 feet that morning when six Zeros jumped us from above. There were five of us, and we worked for altitude. Every time a plane attacked us, we pulled up at him and tried to meet him head on. By this simple maneuver we got up to 6,000 or 7,000 feet, then took them on in a dogfight.

My first job was to take care of a Zero that was on a Marine's tail. I dove after him. He was pretty far away— almost out of range. My bullets went below and off to the side. He was making a turn facing me.

When I fired, it seemed to scare him and he hauled back on the stick, pulling his plane straight up in the air. I was above him, going like hell, and when he started climbing, I pulled up too and got a few yards behind him.

I had the plane in my sights, all ready to shoot, when I saw him crawl out on the right wing. He was hunched over, so close I could see the details of his blackish green gabardine flying suit and his helmet. I couldn't see his face. I wanted to blow the plane out from under him, but he just managed to jump clear as I shot. My fire went right into the tail, traveled the length of the plane, and blew it up. The pilot hurtled by with a swish and I lost sight of him momentarily while the pieces were flying.

Later I saw his chute open and he landed right on our front lines. I never learned what happened to him.

While I was glancing down, I saw a Zero diving at a 45° angle, with flames coming out of it around the motor. It appeared to be torching. The flames seemed to grow bigger and streamed out behind.

The plane was going wide open. As it got down, just before hitting the ground, the pilot pulled out of the dive. A few feet above a flat pasture near the river, east of the field, he hit the ground almost parallel with tremendous speed. There was a great explosion which threw dirt, fire, and pieces of junk in all directions.

I wasted precious ammunition shooting at several distant planes and got what I deserved—clean misses. Then I saw a Zero circling above. As I pulled up and started toward him, he started toward me too. He was right in front of me—huge red dots on each side of his wings and fuselage, his plane a dirty gray below, rust colored on top. On my first short burst, smoke started pouring out of him. He made a frantic turn out over the sea and started to lose altitude. Since I did not want to follow him and leave the rest of my flight, I let him go and watched as he kept smoking and losing altitude till he plunged into the sea.

By this time five of the six Zeros had been shot down and one of our men—Lieutenant Bate—had been forced to bail out due to fire. He landed on the beach and walked safely to the field. It was the first and last Wildcat I ever heard of catching fire. There was actually little fire in this case, but Bate didn't want to take any chances.

The sixth Zero fled. Haberman, Doyle, and I chased him until he pulled into a cloud and lost us. Then I returned to the field and watched dogfights that were just out of range of our anti-aircraft. Those two Zeros, incidentally, were numbers twelve and thirteen for my collection.

At midafternoon my "flying circus"—a name hung on the flight by Colonel Bauer—prepared to take off again to engage a large group of Zeros. The spirit of these boys can be illustrated by Oscar Bate's reaction when he found his name wasn't on the afternoon flight list.

"How come I am not on the schedule?" he demanded of Colonel Bauer. "I am in Captain Foss' flight."

"You've had some trouble, and I'll give you a few days off," said the Colonel.

Bate thrust his chin out. "I'll have you know that just because I got shot down is no sign I can't fly," he roared.

"By God, you're on my ball team," said the Colonel. "I'll put your name on the schedule." And he scratched the name of the substitute and put Bate's name back on.

Ensign Brown, a young naval flyer, was on my wing that day and was hugging fairly close. "I want to see how you do it," he kiddingly said as we took off.

We were able to show him a little excitement. We attacked from above and sneaked up behind the enemy flight, which was unaware we were in the area. They were sailing along with splendid calm and indifference. Our first bursts blew up several of them and crippled others.

With Ensign Brown close by, I was at such close range on my Zero that I narrowly escaped hitting the flying pieces. The motor made an unpredictable gyration, as it always does, and came unpleasantly near getting Brown.

Things weren't so easy after that. We were in a melee and several Zeros made enthusiastic runs on me before I could do anything about it. Then came one, like a maniac, with a high-diving run. I laughed to myself, for his bullets were going far below. As he started to pass, I made a right turn, swung onto his tail, and gave him a liberal treatment. He blew up with a sky-shaking roar. The pilot popped out, apparently unhurt, and started hitchhiking down to earth.

By that time we were pretty close to the field, and ammunition and gasoline were low. The boys went in and started landing. I circled wide toward the mountains before coming in and looked around closely. It was a good thing I did. A lonesome Grumman was coming toward the field. Behind him two Zeros were sneaking in. "All men in this area," I barked anxiously into my radio, "look out for Zeros. Look out—they're sneaking up on you."

The Grumman seemed to pay no attention. A Zero slid down within a hundred feet of its tail before letting go with all its guns. The Grumman was almost blown out of the air. It fell into a spin for the ground. The Zero went into a triumphant slow roll of celebration.

The two enemy planes were between me and the field, and I had little gas or ammunition. I headed for a cloud, hoping they wouldn't spot me. But they did, and swung right along behind.

I went into one cloud, popped out the other side, and ducked into the next, tipping the Grumman's nose up to get a little altitude and circling around. I was on top of the cloud and going in the opposite direction when I saw my two little friends below. Each had gone around the second cloud, expecting me to come out the other end. Instead, they only met each other.

Giving up the chase, they started away. I was able to slip down onto the tail of the nearest. I eased up to within a few feet and blew him into a million little jagged worthless pieces with one burst. The guns delivered only a few rounds before they quit—I was out of ammunition. If it hadn't been for that, I could have had the second plane. But the remaining Zero had no disposition to make a fight of it. He wheeled for Tokyo for all he was worth, and I made for Henderson Field just as fast. It was six or seven miles away, and I was in a hurry.

I found the man who had been shot down in the Grumman had miraculously escaped death. Luckily, he had been able to pull out of his spin and bring the plane down.

Ensign Brown was also congratulating himself on a narrow escape from death. "You don't fight fair," he kidded me. "You get up so close to the Zeros that it would be impossible for anybody to miss. Why, you actually leave powder burns on 'em."

I told him such details were unimportant so long as we kept junk falling from the sky.

Those five new Zeros brought my score to sixteen. Our tally for the day was seven Zeros and five reconnaissance bombers. All squadrons combined got nineteen Zeros and five bombers, plus the two destroyers of course.

"That was one hop I didn't get any bullet holes in my plane," I told Danny Doyle later.

He looked at me queerly. "What do you call those?" he inquired, pointing to my headrest.

It had been hit plenty. That was the only time I was ever hit on the headrest.

•

CHAPTER VIII

Y

THE JAPS DID SOME QUEER THINGS SOMETIMES. I DON'T KNOW whether you'd call it bravery or foolishness.

Early one day a Mitsubishi reconnaissance bomber—a slick-looking, two-engined job that moves along pretty fast —came over Guadalcanal and took pictures. Our anti-aircraft fired and missed.

The Jap circled wide, then dove and came in, apparently to strafe the field and prove how much nerve he had. He roared impudently down the runway almost on the ground, and every man on the field that could lay his hand on a pistol, rifle, or .50-caliber machine gun cut loose at him from foxholes. Several hits were scored—I saw some on the wings especially.

Anyway, the bomber did a steep wingover, drove straight into the ground behind the trees and exploded. Pieces of three bodies were found and no more. I saw one of our men trying to get a boot off a leg for a souvenir. Others found a .32 Colt revolver and a saber in the wreckage.

78

Our boys developed an amused contempt for Jap flyers, at the same time respecting the Zero for its good qualities. On the ground we looked up and laughed as the enemy showed off by putting on an aerial circus. "Look at the crazy dopes!" was our response to the slow rolls, wingovers and intricate loops.

With all their sophomoric aerobatics the Zeros reminded me of dogs running across the fields on a spring day. One raced in front with his tongue hanging out, and the others followed, doing wingovers and loops and all sorts of crazy things. They wandered all over the sky, never assembling in formations.

Because of uninspired tactical training, they passed up a lot of good chances in combat—chances our boys knew how to cash in on. They seemed to be following some kind of secret code which allowed of no deviation, like a system for beating the bank at Monte Carlo. Our tactics, on the other hand, were completely elastic; we were always improvising.

But you couldn't laugh at the Zero itself. In its peculiar way, it was the best fighting plane in the world at that time. It had our Wildcats beat in interception, maneuverability, climb, and speed. It could turn on a dime, and it could climb like a scared monkey on a rope. I could take any one of my pilots and put him in a Zero, and he would shoot hell out of me in no time.

But actually, of course, none of our boys cared to ride in a Zero. They were too vulnerable. Hit right, they exploded or torched. Our Grummans were almost completely proof against fire and explosion. They were also well armored. Back of the seat was heavy protective armor, cut the shape of a man and capable of stopping anything the Japs threw at us. This was a very comforting feature in a dogfight. The Grummans had superior firepower too—more than we really needed. Six converging streams of .50-caliber bullets, fired by a delicate trigger on the control stick, ripped apart anything they touched. Often I conserved ammunition by cutting out two guns and using only four. We learned the value of going easy on ammunition—running out at critical times cost me at least four planes which were helpless in my sights at one time or another.

We worked out many combat tactics for ourselves on Guadalcanal, adding them to the solid foundation we got in school, and from talking to veteran naval pilots who had seen action earlier in the war. We soon learned the value of working in close before doing our shooting. We got better results that way.

We also got wise to the value of little things—such as keeping our planes clean inside and out. Dirt on the outside cuts knots off a ship's speed. It also conceals bullet holes and mechanical faults that otherwise would be as plain as the teeth in a Jap's face. Inside, dirt is dangerous because in maneuvering a pilot might get an eyeful right in the middle of a dogfight. The windshield, particularly, should be spotless.

Colonel Bauer had a positive, hard-hitting philosophy of air combat that always tickled me. Many of his ideas have since been incorporated into the new manuals. He formed his theories on the spot at Guadalcanal from watching combat results and questioning us when we returned from fights.

I can see him yet as he pounded those ideas home untiringly. "A successful fighter pilot must be aggressive. . . . He

Joe, third from left, called these Guadalcanal veterans "my boys."

These were Joe's flight mates. Left to right standing: Lt. Oscar Bate, Essex Falls, N. J.; Capt. Gregory K. Loesch, Montrose, Colorado; Lt. Thomas Furlow, Ogden, Ark.; Lt. Roger Haberman, Ellsworth, Wisconsin; Lt. William Freeman, Bonham, Texas, and Captain Foss. Kneeling: Lt. William Marontate, Seattle, Wash.; Lt. Frank Presley, Encinitas, Calif.

On Guadalcanal, Joe grew a beard and appeared customarily in his old
hunting cap. Other pilots wore baseball caps.

is not the kind of a man who will turn tail and run. Pilots
who do that get their rear extremities full of arrows. . . . We
must all realize the Zero pilot isn't such a smart guy, or he
would take better advantage of his speed, climb, and maneuverability. . . . Our pilots must avoid getting separated
from formations at all costs. We'll have to give them credit
—the Japs have a deadly way of knocking down stragglers.

"Aim for the wing base on all Japanese planes. That's the
best target. None of their planes has armor or self-sealing
tanks. . . .

"Be an aggressor. Your job is to shoot down Japanese
planes. Outsmart the enemy. You should have complete
faith in your armor and confidence in your ability to shoot
down any plane you see when you get it in your sights. . . .

"So you want a safe war? There's no way to make war
safe. The thing for you to do is to make it very UNSAFE
for the enemy."

I am not revealing a tactical secret when I say we grew
fond of going at the Zeros head on, as if attempting to ram
them. The superior ruggedness of our Wildcats made this
possible. Japs knew a collision was suicide and were also
afraid of our devastating firepower. On a head-on approach
we usually got a good shot, too, when the Zero slow rolled,
looped, or made a climbing turn to avoid our attack.

Tail shots, of course, were most productive of results when
we could surprise the Zeros. Deflection shooting, from the
side, was a difficult test of marksmanship. It amuses me to
read reports that this is a "new science." It is as old as air
fighting itself—in fact it's the same thing as shooting a
pheasant on the fly.

The Jap attacks developed a more or less regular pattern.

High-level bombers were always escorted by Zeros, the number varying from half a dozen to two dozen, apparently dependent on the number they had on hand. Most of the escort force came in several thousand feet above the bombardment formation, but there was always a smaller group somewhere around, doing playful maneuvers and loops. The reason for this eccentric behavior we never knew—maybe they did it so they could keep watch in all directions. Often the Zeros left cloud trails which remained in the sky like insolent messages for several minutes.

How the enemy replaced his plane losses was a mystery. Certainly they were heavy. Yet he sent his Zeros over almost endlessly. After a time the strain showed, not in planes but in pilots. They were obviously less experienced, less well-grounded in tactics. "The second team," Marines called them.

On the twenty-sixth of October, anti-aircraft gunners pointed out with some pride that they had shot down twenty-six planes during the month—one for every day. This was roughly one for every eight shot down by fighter planes and represented a highly effective showing. The virtuosity of these gunners, many of them veterans of Pearl Harbor and Midway, took a heavy load off our shoulders. Don't think we didn't appreciate it.

Big booms from the ground fighting kept us awake during this dangerous period. On Monday no Jap planes showed up—the enemy stayed home licking his wounds of the day before. Again I walked up to the front lines to see the good Japs—dead ones—that had collected overnight.

After a big battle, ground troops had Jap flags, sabers, money, pistols, rifles, and pictures to trade. Pilots used candy, cigarettes, cigars, even watches, for trading stock. Money had little value. One flyer gave a can of chicken, a can of beans, and a towel for a Jap rifle. Most of the men had bracelets made of metal from fallen Zeros.

The disposal of enemy dead was such a problem that engineers blasted a cliff near the Matanikau River to cover a heap of bodies at its foot. Captured Jap equipment included flame throwers, mortars, anti-tank guns, and devices for purifying water. Most significant, however, were American tommy guns of a type used on Bataan. That made our boys see red.

For hours I talked with Captain Ben Finney of New York City about hunting. Many of the pilots were young men who loved hunting. To them Zeros were just like ducks—except that they shot back. Ben told of his big-game hunting trips all over the world, and I talked about South Dakota ducks, pheasants, and the trapping out there. We talked endlessly about guns, which I love.

It wasn't until later that we heard of the big naval air battle off the Santa Cruz Islands. This had an important bearing on the defense of Guadalcanal. It was expensive for both sides—we lost the *Hornet,* and the Japs lost 104 planes besides some ships. But for our side it was worth the cost. The appearance of two Jap task forces off the Stewart Islands and the New Hebrides October 26 was a screening action to permit battleships to move in for a second bombardment of our positions, while land forces made a grand mass assault.

The Jap troops on Guadalcanal fought bravely and well, but their naval forces and flyers let them down. The battle of Santa Cruz wrecked one part of the plan by putting their warships to flight. We were able to do our share by giving a decisive beating to their air support at a time when it was critically needed. I don't think they counted on the toughness of our ground troops, either. Between October 22 and 27 they lost 2,000 men in attacks which gained no ground. On that latter date, on an island twenty-five miles wide and eighty-five miles long, we occupied a little stretch only three miles deep and six miles long.

That day, for the last time, Jap attacks pierced our lines south of the airfield. Again the enemy was driven back. Artillery shells dropped here and there on the field. Our planes bombed enemy gun positions west of the field, destroying an AA battery and an ammunition dump.

With the backbone of the enemy attack broken, both sides were glad of a breathing spell, and the remainder of October was quiet. Small flights of Zeros came over occasionally. Eight were knocked down one day with the loss of one plane for us.

Another day we went to meet an enemy flight but it turned and fled, so no contact was made. The Japs had grown timid after our big week end. Sometimes high-altitude bombers came over during the night or early in the morning.

Twice Marine flights raided the Jap base at Rekata Bay. The first time four float biplanes and two Zero floats were found on the water. Four of them were left burning and the others so riddled as to be useless.

Two days later Colonel Bauer (he was called "the Coach" by the team-minded pilots) lined up a surprise attack. Arriving at 4:15, just as dawn was lifting, a flight led by Cowboy Stout found the bay covered with float monoplanes and biplanes. "Let 'em get up off the water," the Cowboy commanded. "Then we can count 'em in our score." Our flyers, I might explain, do not count planes destroyed on the ground or water.

In fierce action over the bay Conger got a monoplane and a biplane. Three others bagged a Zero apiece. Stout happened to be first back at the field. He was sad as ship after ship came in. "They got one of our boys," he said. "I saw a Grumman crash headlong into the water with a Zero on its tail."

Soon all the Grummans were back. Stout was amazed. The only explanation was that one Zero had shot another down in the darkness.

Drury was exasperated when he found his wings laced with .50-caliber bullet holes. "What are you guys trying to do?" he raved. "Kill me?"

The morning's work brought Conger's combat score to ten planes and half a destroyer. The Coach had ten planes and a "smoker" which he had not seen crash and characteristically refused to count. These were the best scores in that squadron. Captain Everton had eight planes, the missing Tex Hamilton seven, Major Payne six, Stout and Drury five apiece, and the others lesser numbers. Lieutenant Dick Haring, Muskegon, Michigan, had been killed without claiming a victim, and Chamberlain, shot down twice and wounded once, likewise had a clean slate. The squadron score was ninety-one planes.

After dark every night we all sat on benches around a square table in the bivouac area, smoking, telling stories, and drinking sparingly of whisky, brandy, strong Australian beer, or fruit juice—whichever was available, in that order of preference. Relaxed, the men turned in from eight to eleven o'clock, as they chose. Nobody read at night. There were few flashlights. Nightly blackouts were not observed, but if approaching planes were heard, every light was doused in an instant.

The question of what we were fighting for never was raised in those sessions around the table at night, but there were plenty of indirect answers. The boys had different reasons. Haberman wanted to "go home, lie around, and listen to the grass grow" in Wisconsin. Brandon wanted to get the Japs licked so he could go home and hunt deer. Loesch and Freeman liked the idea of deer hunting, too, but added trout fishing to their list.

Some of the other boys had different ideas—they were fighting for personal satisfaction, for fun, or for lower taxes. But mostly they just wanted to go home, get married, and continue doing the things they'd always enjoyed.

It was pretty much that way with me. I wanted to help keep my country the way it was—a place where some day June and I could own a ranch and live the way we wanted to, working, hunting, fishing, and maybe some day rearing a little family.

Outside of combat there were few high spots in our lives. A letter from home, a sliver of ice from the ten-pound cake the ice plant disgorged each night, a shower to ease the intolerable heat, a gratifying news bulletin from the wireless —these were minor climaxes of existence.

In the absence of dogfights the big events were such things as the arrival of fresh meat or beer. When we had steak for evening chow, it called for a celebration. Once my flight of eight got five bottles of beer, brought off a ship. Some boys don't like that Australian beer, but I do. It has some body to it.

On visits to the front lines, I often marveled at the endurance of our ground fighters. Sometimes the smell of rotting enemy bodies was past description. When bodies lay in front of dense jungle, they could not be reached for burial, because snipers would pick off anyone who approached.

I went hunting for snipers with some of the boys, in spite of Colonel Bauer's objection. "Too dangerous!" he snorted—a remark that made us laugh. It was a hot day—so sultry that I came near passing out. I became separated from the rest and soon heard one of the men cut loose with his tommy gun. I yelled and asked if he had anything. He said he saw a bush move but did not see anything. That was enough for me—I left. This was about two hundred yards from the field.

Snipers often slipped through the lines and fired at our mechanics at work on the field. Many of these Japs were terrible shots, but sometimes our mechanics would get sore, grab up guns, and take to the woods for a sniper hunt.

One big husky fellow with the build of a wrestler—we called him "Dude"—didn't bother to take a gun. He slipped into the woods one day after being fired on too many times. He found the Jap and killed him with a knife. When he returned, he had an entire Jap outfit, and he was covered with blood as if he had butchered a hog.

CHAPTER IX

Y

DEATH SEEMED ALWAYS JUST AROUND THE CORNER, WAITING patiently to capitalize on a moment's carelessness or bad luck. One night, for example, we took off at dusk to intercept enemy planes, but failed to find them. We returned after dark, in blinding rain.

A plane from another flight ran out of gas and stalled over my head. The pilot—Ensign "Red" Thrash, as I learned later—bailed out. His chute bloomed directly before me, and I barely managed to clear it with a wing. The plane dropped in front of me and spun to the beach, where it exploded and burned with a red glow.

A little bad luck might have taken two lives that night. It was raining so hard we could just make out the boundary lights of the field as we landed.

With death and injury daily occurrences we didn't talk about them much. When a good friend failed to return, we tightened our jaws and said nothing. The boys developed a fatalistic slant. "If your number's up, you're going to get it even if you're in a bombproof ten feet underground," was the way one flyer put it. Anybody who brooded about dying out there was due to go off his rocker. Few of the boys read *Bibles,* but all of us thought more about religion.

Guadalcanal was not a place for heroes or glamour boys. As a matter of fact, the very word "hero" turned our stomachs, especially when applied to us. It still does with me. We were frequently scared and admitted it. Once Bob Cromie, the *Chicago Tribune* correspondent, asked me if I were frightened during my first battle. My answer was short and true:

"Hell, yes!"

Anybody who says he isn't scared when bullets start tearing through his plane is obviously a liar. But a man must be able to conquer that fear somehow; the fellow who stays scared doesn't belong in the business. A sky filled with enemy planes is no spot for weak sisters.

We learned that men who had been athletic stars didn't necessarily turn out to be good fighting men. Some were great, of course. But others were failures. We had to send two of them home. They didn't have what it takes. This made me think of something once said by my old coach at the University of South Dakota, "Rube" Hoy: "A boy doesn't need to be a star," he said, "as long as he gets the idea of teamwork and sportsmanship." Rube, a philosopher and wit as well as a gentleman, thought as much of a boy who never got his name in the paper as he did of a star.

The Jap absenteeism continued for a time as November opened. Sitting and waiting began to get us down. One day we tried to make ourselves useful by bombing Jap concentrations east of the field. We hooked bombs on our Grummans and suitably greeted, from treetop level, Jap soldiers who had landed the night before near Koli point. From our altitude we didn't need to worry much about the bombs being delivered to the proper address.

There was rain and more rain. The cool nights made perfect sleeping weather. Sometimes we went out into the rain before going to bed and enjoyed a cool shower. Our troops started a push to the northwest and met with little resistance. They gained two miles. We received word that the squadron would soon be sent away from Guadalcanal for a rest.

The score sheet for October showed 369 enemy planes destroyed, bringing the total for the campaign to 520.

It seemed good to see new troops coming in. On November 4 we threw a protective patrol over the harbor while ships unloaded. They had crept in under cover of darkness early in the morning. As daylight broke, the transports steamed in close to shore and the warships fanned out in the surrounding waters. Unloading operations continued smoothly until almost noon, when Japanese planes appeared in the distance. They were easily driven off, and the transports, which had steamed out to join the destroyers, returned and continued unloading.

That night the ships were protected by torpedo boats. Unloading was resumed in the morning. At 9:15 A.M. we received a report that twenty-seven Japanese high-altitude bombers and fighters were headed our way. The transports again interrupted unloading while we went up to intercept the attack.

It was a gray day with about nine layers of clouds. We climbed and looked between one cloud layer and then another, as if we were searching, floor by floor, a huge warehouse in the sky.

My first sight of the enemy came when I saw the shattered fuselage of a bomber going by me, straight for the ground. Anti-aircraft gunners knocked down five bombers and a Zero from that enemy flight. The sight of all those falling pieces going past scared us plenty. The bombers never reached the harbor, but dropped their loads in the jungle, far away.

We tore through all the clouds and never saw any other trace of enemy planes. The ground gunners were the whole show that day. It made them feel better. They had complained that on the four previous days Jap planes had been unable to get within firing distance of the field, and the AA crews were getting rusty.

The ships in the harbor completed their unloading without the loss of a man or piece of equipment.

When we returned to the field, Captain Finney had a weird story to tell. Watching the falling bomber fragments with his glasses, he had spotted the back half of a fuselage coming down with one man trapped in it. The fuselage was like a tube with both ends blown out, and Captain Finney could see this thing spinning over and over all the way down, with this man vainly trying to escape. He went right in and never did get out.

A few hours later, Lieutenant Grow, who had been missing for several weeks, calmly walked into camp. He really had a lot to tell, but in his quiet way he said little, and we had to ask endless questions to get any dope out of him. He had been shot down—his motor was shot out—and he landed offshore behind the Jap lines.

He thought he was close to shore but had a long, exhausting swim before reaching it. He gave up hope several times and nearly drowned. When he got to the beach, he went to sleep, not caring who got him—crocodile or Jap.

When he woke up, a native was standing over him with a big club. Grow started to get up, and the native disappeared in the jungle. Grow just crawled into the brush, hid, and went back to sleep.

The natives found him and led him to a mission when he said he was an American. A father took care of him, nursed him back to health, and allowed him to live at the mission, which was on the other side of Guadalcanal.

Grow went crocodile hunting with the padre but didn't get any. The padre did, though. The natives demonstrated how sharks would attack things by throwing a cat in and watching the sharks take it. Grow learned a lot about native life before he returned to our lines.

Two more missing boys came back that night. One of them was Lieutenant Dale M. Leslie, twenty-five, of Madison, Florida, a dive bomber who had been lost for several weeks in the jungle behind the lines. The other was Lieutenant Wallace L. Dinn, of Corpus Christi, Texas, an Army pilot who had been shot down on another island. When he came back, he brought a Zero pilot along as prisoner.

Dinn had a good story. He was on a mission when the Jap attacked him. Both planes were badly damaged and had to make crash landings. Both pilots were injured. But Dinn enlisted the help of friendly natives and captured the Jap. Marine scouts later found and returned him and his Jap to Guadalcanal.

Missing pilots often made their way back through the Jap lines, something that gave us hope whenever men failed to return. Marion Carl did it, long before, and so did Smitty.

Carl was mourned for five days before he walked out of the jungle.

It developed that he bailed out near an island and found a native in an old motorboat. Nursing this frail craft along, they got back to the small area of Guadalcanal then occupied by Americans. Those were the days when Carl was trying to catch up with Smitty in number of planes shot down. He went right up to the commanding general and asked that Major Smith be grounded for five days. "It isn't fair, general," he complained. "How can I catch up with him now?"

Smith was shot down a little later six miles inside Jap-held territory. He struck out through the woods, fording rivers, and got back to the field in two and one-half hours. He didn't see a Jap. "It was just like taking a hike," he said.

Lieutenant Chamberlain of 212 once showed up after an absence of six days. He had been marooned on a little island off to the northeast, where he lived on coconuts.

Staff Sergeant James Feliton, a flyer from Syracuse, New York, came back in triumph, surrounded by a whole tribe of grinning natives, after being forced to parachute thirty miles behind the lines. He was missing three days.

Japs blew him out of a flight of Grummans at 20,000 feet. His cockpit was badly shot up and oil spurted into his face. Something hit him on the back of the head and just about knocked him out. He managed to get away, but a panel ripped out of his chute, and he landed hard in some bushes. Bruised and lacerated, he lay in the chute all night.

Then he started back through the jungle, using a compass to keep from wandering in circles. He encountered several natives, who had been driven into the backwoods by Japs, but they ran away.

Finally the whole tribe, well-armed, came after him, intending to knock him off. But Feliton hadn't been an insurance salesman in private life for nothing. Soon he had them eating out of his hand. One native, who spoke broken English, turned out to be a special friend.

The natives took him to their village, fed him papaya, pineapple, French-fried yams and beef, bathed him, then gave him the chief's hut to sleep in. Next morning they gave him a royal escort for the trip back. Feliton was passed from village to village by friendly natives. He was surrounded by fully thirty natives when the long trek ended at the airfield.

We loaded the tribesmen down with presents—all the cans of Spam they could carry, cigarettes, peanuts, and an axe, which they specially valued.

Early November continued quiet, except for ground action. In the western sector our boys killed 350 Japs and captured three field pieces, a dozen 37-mm. guns, and thirty machine guns.

Maytag Charlie continued his desultory bombing at night. Usually his eggs' landed far away. The arrival of supplies relieved us of worry about gasoline and other necessities. We spent a long time, just sitting and waiting. Squadron 212 left the island after forty-three days of action altogether. Rog Haberman went to another island to get his teeth fixed. A sniper got loose in the neighborhood of the camp and raised hell.

CHAPTER X

Y

"... HOWEVER, FOUR OF THE AMERICAN PLANES FAILED TO return." Excerpt from Associated Press dispatch, Guadalcanal, November 7, 1942.

One of those missing planes was mine.

I will never forget November 7. It began quietly. Scorekeepers on the ground put in their time adding up Japanese losses since our first landing on the island. By actual count enemy bodies numbered 5,188. The battle line now ran from Point Cruz on the west to Koli Point on the east—about 12¼ miles.

In the afternoon we were ordered to attack a small Japanese force of ten destroyers and a light cruiser, steaming toward us from about 150 miles to the north. Just as we sighted them, I saw six float Zeros in front of us, about a thousand feet below. They were going in the same direction we were, shooting at another flight of Wildcats led by Major Paul Fontana, of Sparks, Nevada. The funny thing

95

about it was that Major Fontana, who did not know he was being fired on, was a couple of thousand feet above me. The Jap pilots were about 3,000 feet from their target, and I could see no sense in wasting ammunition at that range.

I called the boys and said, "Don't look now, but I think we have something here." We immediately started down for the attack. It was a mad race. All of us—we had seven planes on that flight—realized there were only six Zeros and somebody was going to get left out. On the way down everybody was trying to pull up, get in there, and get a shot.

Boot Furlow practically climbed under my wing. When I shot, the first short burst blew the Zero into a thousand pieces. The motor went off on a tangent and Boot, in order to avoid hitting it, had to do a Houdini.

I went in the other direction. As I came in again, Boot had already got on the tail of a second plane and shot it down flaming. I thought I would do a quick wingover and get another shot but by that time the six Zeros were all blown to pieces. Aside from dropping fragments—and chutes—we were alone in the sky.

Five of the chutes, strangely enough, were empty. Above me about 2,000 feet hung the sixth with an enemy pilot dangling in the harness. At that moment the Jap unbuckled himself and jumped out. He passed me on his back, falling head-first at a little angle. Seconds later he hit the sea and threw up a big geyser of water.

The other five flyers had apparently done the same, although none of us actually saw them. The reasons for such suicidal tactics were a mystery. I never saw either side shoot at a parachuting man in the Guadalcanal area.

One of the boys: Major Jack Cram,
of Seattle, Washington.

Lt. Col. Sam Jack, fighter commander at Guadalcanal.
This picture was taken just after Col. Joe Bauer,
Coronado, Calif., failed to return from a mission.

The flight on its second trip to Guadalcanal. Left to right: Haberman, Freeman, Furlow, Foss, Loesch, Presley, Marontate and Bate.

We went on with our attack, my boys joining up with Major Fontana's flight in reverse order, since we were going in to strafe the ships. That made me the tail-ender. Before I went down, I followed a useful custom and scanned the clouds. Caution paid dividends once more. The float of a scout plane was protruding from a cloud.

"You better get this baby so he won't follow you down in your dive and be dangerous," I told myself. I circled and made a diving run on him as if he had been a Zero. But he was a single-motored scout biplane, almost stationary up there high above the sea. Before I knew it, I was too close to shoot and had to worry about missing him.

I came down from behind, flipped over on my side, and squeezed by. As I passed, he turned over on his side too, and the rear gunner cut loose with his free gun. My plane was hit several times. One bullet splintered through the left side of the hood and out the curved part of the cockpit glass, right in front of my face.

This made a good-sized hole. The wind howling through it scared hell out of me. Seeing there was nothing specially wrong, however, I soon quieted down and circled for a diving belly shot.

My bullets hit the right wing just below the fuselage, sending the plane into a crazy spin. I left it. The last I saw it was hurtling toward the sea. A second craft of the same type—somewhat like our navy SOCs—was coming in, not seeing me. I circled for position behind him, pulled up, and made an unhurried belly shot. He was an accommodating cuss—he burst into flames at once and went torching into the sea.

The planes of that day were later credited as numbers seventeen, eighteen, and nineteen on my list.

It was time to look for my boys. I had made the mistake of leaving my flight to get those last two planes and was afraid of being hopped by Zeros and shot down. The straggler is usually on his last mission unless he happens to be really lucky. I looked down at the ships in the vicinity. The Jap cruiser had been hit hard and was apparently in a bad way. A destroyer had also taken a beating. But there was no sign of our planes—they had done their chores and were long since gone.

Finally, though, I spotted another fighter. Pulling up alongside him, I gave the join-up signal. When he did not join up, I kept on going. I later learned he was having motor trouble and his plane could go no faster.

I was on the way home alone. Ahead were several rain squalls—just like waterfalls in the sky. Confident of the way, I didn't bother to check my compass. When I did, I was 30° off course. I saw a big squall directly ahead and figured if I went to the left of it, I would come right between the two big islands that stand as a gateway to Guadalcanal.

Instead, I should have gone to the right. The rain was covering the island I was aiming for. When the plane was turning and abreast of the rain squall, my motor started fading and throwing out clouds of smoke. I tried my best to push it along—you know, the way a child leans forward and pushes a kiddie car to get every foot. By this time it was apparent that the island wasn't anywhere near Guadalcanal. I was far off the route. In a moment the motor quit, caught hold again, then conked out cold. I tell you my hair stood up so straight it raised the helmet right off my head.

There was only one thing to do. I glided on, trying to make every inch I could toward the island. I could have turned at one point and landed close to shore, but I made a foolish circle in the wrong direction and landed between two and five miles offshore. That's a long way when you are strictly a fresh-water swimmer.

The tail hooked into the water, the plane skipped, hit with a solid smack the second time, nosed over like a brick, and went down instantly, nose first. Water poured in so fast it almost knocked me out. I had forgotten to pull the leg straps on the chute. When the water came in, the buoyancy of the chute and my Mae West floated me up. I was really buoyant. Trying to get the leg strap off, I bent my foot back, but it went under the seat and caught, so I was unable to get loose.

In my excitement I took in a couple of gulps of salt water. I stopped and thought the thing over there, thirty feet under the surface. "Listen, dope," I told myself, "if you don't quiet down, there isn't going to be any show." Using almost the last of my strength, I pulled down against the unwelcome buoyancy and managed to get my foot out. The water seemed to be crushing me as I shot to the surface.

Still the leg straps on the chute were buckled. They pulled me around and dumped me with my fanny up and my face down in the water. I had a tough time getting the straps unbuckled and the Mae West out of the way. In the process I swallowed several more gulps of sea water. The life jacket came up to my ears and almost got away.

By the time I had everything fixed okay, my shoes felt too heavy, so I pulled them off and let them sink. There I was, thrashing about in the water. I wasn't sure I stood any chance. It looked like it was about the end of the jig.

I don't say my thoughts would have made a three-dollar book, but plenty of things went through my mind as I looked toward shore. The current was so strong my best efforts only kept me in the same spot. I wondered what my wife would think when I didn't come back. I wondered if she would ever find out where I went and what became of me, and I wondered what the boys back at camp would say. I would swear that twice shark fins cut the water a few feet away. It was a horrible feeling.

I did more praying that afternoon out there than I ever did in my life. "Poor old Joe finally got it," I could imagine the boys saying. "He's shark bait." Every time I put out my arm to swim, I expected to draw back a stub. After a while I thought of the chlorine capsule in my pocket and broke it for protection. It seemed to keep the sharks—if any— away.

I continued splashing hopelessly. In an hour or so it was dark. I was heading for a point that looked close, but the longer I swam the farther away it seemed. In the dark I could see glowing phosphorescent patches in the water. I thought they were made by sharks' fins, and they nearly scared me to death.

After a while I could hear canoes coming toward me. There was the splash of paddles and a low mumble of conversation, but I could hear nothing else. Afraid of Japs, I kept still in the water as the canoes came straight toward me. I feared the paddlers would hear even my breath. They came so close I was between an outrigger and its canoe for a moment. As they missed me by inches I didn't move—just rolled my eyes in the dark, trying to make out who was in the canoes.

One man some distance away had a lantern. After the canoes had circled and hunted for about thirty minutes, the man with the lantern yelled, "Let's look over 'ere." Those were about the most welcome words I ever heard. "Yeah, over here!" I sang out. The men in the closest canoe just about bailed out, they were so surprised. The fellow with the lantern rowed over and circled, holding the light on me doubtfully and sizing me up. Silent faces in the shadows seemed to say, "If you turn out to be somebody we don't like, we'll bash your brains out." I did plenty of talking to convince them I was a good friend of theirs.

Finally they pulled me aboard, apparently satisfied, and whistled across the water to friends ashore. One of the men—a planter—had seen me land on the water.

I still had my chute with me. By this time its buoyancy was reduced to practically nothing. It was badly water-logged and weighed several pounds. As the men pulled it into the boat with difficulty, one remarked, "You must be a superman to drag anything like that along with you."

They paddled rapidly and after a little bit swung into double time. I sat facing the man who had hauled me out—he turned out to be Tommy, a sawmill owner. He was holding his lantern up, when . . . Bam! . . . something hit the lantern and dropped into the boat. It was a fish resembling a gar, about twenty inches long and with a long, sharp bill like a needle. Tommy quickly ducked the lantern. "I should have kept this thing down," he apologized, "but

I guess I got a little excited. Plenty of men have lost their eyes at night because of holding lights. These jumping fish pierced their eyes." From then on in, I held my hands over my face and peeked through my fingers. I was in no mood to lose an eye.

Tommy said I was lucky not to reach the point I had been aiming for so unsuccessfully. I would have landed on a peninsula and walked across it, fording a stagnant stream to reach the mainland. That stream was filled with man-eating crocodiles. No doubt I would have walked right into the mouth of one of these cheerful customers.

This turned out to be Malaita Island, and there was a mission on it. All the padres were gathered on the beach as a welcoming committee. They had been out in canoes looking for me too. There were two bishops, four fathers, two brothers, and eight sisters. Besides Tommy, the sawmill owner, there was a Norwegian planter. It was a regular League of Nations. One bishop was a Frenchman, the other a Russian. One father was from the Netherlands, another from Australia, still another from Norway. A brother was from Emmetsburg, Iowa, and another was from Italy. A sister was from Boston. The others came from as many different countries as the fathers.

They gave me some dry clothing. I gave my old clothes to the natives. Most of these missionaries had come here from other islands where the Japs were now in charge, and the same was true of the nuns. The Japs had an ugly habit of bayoneting missionaries through the throat.

That night I dined better than I ever had on Guadalcanal —steak (the first fresh meat I'd seen in weeks), eggs, papaya, pineapple. We sat up and talked till almost midnight. They wanted to know what was going on in the world, how the war was progressing, what was happening at Guadalcanal. Their only news came from Tommy, who had a little radio set aboard his scow. He tuned in the news every night, listened intently, and then came over to report. Though the war was going on right in their back yard, these people knew little except what they could see. One sister had been there forty years and had never seen an automobile. The first airplanes she saw were warplanes over the islands.

The missionaries had no tobacco other than that grown on the island, and this tasted like a poor brand of straw. I resolved to fly over with a sack of tobacco the first thing after returning to Guadalcanal. One of the fathers gave me his bed for the night. It was a woven job—thatch mat with a half-inch pad—and a pillow that resembled a hundred-pound sack of rock salt. But it was the best he had, and hard as it was I slept as if it had been a "Beautyrest" mattress. There was only one interruption. In the middle of the night I got up to be sick from the salt water I had swallowed.

Early the next morning, Sunday, I was awakened by singing. I got up and found my way to a little thatched church with a dirt floor. Services were underway, and the singing— a kind of weird howling would describe it better—was the chanting of the natives. It was an amazing thing. All the women were up in front and a padre was leading the song. I don't know what language he was using—I couldn't understand it. But it certainly sounded good. The altar was of bamboo and coconut shells. The natives, who were some of the orneriest characters in the entire Solomon Islands, wore red loincloths and their mouths were dripping red from betel nut.

After church I was placed on review—my first public appearance on any stage. The fathers asked me to stand in the covered areaway between two houses while the natives passed by and looked me over. They were great powerful brutes with bushy hair and savage faces, and they looked at me wonderingly, as if I were some strange animal. One of them was wearing my pants—given away the night before —and another was wearing my shirt.

A father explained their amazement. Many years before the war, an American schooner had stopped at Malaita with a crew of southern Negroes. They had told the natives they were Americans, so the natives expected to find me black.

We had a fine breakfast. Everything on the table was strictly the fat of the land, even though no supplies had been received for thirteen months. With arrival of the extra fathers and sisters, the food problem must have grown acute. But that morning we had eggs—a dessert to me—fresh goat's milk, and a dark bread that was really good, plus papaya and some delicious fruit I could not identify. In my honor we each had two slices of bread. Bread had been rationed, one slice per man.

The fathers pressed me to stay for two weeks. I agreed to stay maybe one week. In the midst of this unprecedented hospitality it looked as if I could get in some fishing, and then there were some wrecked Jap bombers and Zeros up in the hills that we intended to check over.

Through the jungle grapevine came word that on the previous day Marine raiders had made a surprise attack on a small Jap camp—a hundred miles away—on Malaita, killing twenty-four Japs and sending the twenty-fifth into the jungle with a slug in his chest.

After breakfast I went out and stretched my chute in the sun to dry. Shortly thereafter the natives started yelling that a plane was coming. Sure enough, a Wildcat soon appeared overhead. The pilot, who turned out later to be Lieutenant Otto Brueggeman, twenty-four, of Lexington, Missouri, spotted the chute. We thought he did, anyway. Then the plane left.

Hours later as we were eating dinner in the dining hall—a small shack about ten feet long and eight feet wide, perched on stilts five or six feet above the ground—we heard the natives shrieking again. We jumped up and ran out. They were looking out under the trees far over the water and said there was a plane coming. Listening, we could neither see nor hear a plane.

But a PBY soon loafed into view. It came over, circled a couple of times, and landed in a little bayou in front of the mission. I hurriedly said my farewells, leaving the silk parachute for the nuns to work up into clothing, and jumped into a canoe powered by two huge natives. Everyone turned out to see me go. Even the nuns left their confines—something one of the fathers said he had never seen happen before.

The PBY was taxiing around in the bayou. Rowing wide open, the natives managed to catch it and I struggled aboard. Inside I found Major Charles Parker of New Orleans, Louisiana, an operations officer. Up ahead at the controls was my old friend, Major Jack Cram.

We took off and flew back to Guadalcanal—me wearing

old socks, no shoes, a baggy pair of white pants, "b.v.d.'s" and a beard.

I went directly to the fighter ready tent and had a grand reunion with my boys. They told me fifteen Jap planes had been shot down the day I got three.

CHAPTER XI

Υ

ALL ALONG I'VE BEEN TRYING TO GIVE YOU AN IDEA OF THE kind of men we had on our side at Guadalcanal. Maybe it would help if I told the story of Casey Brandon and Danny Doyle, two of my boys that didn't come back.

Casey was an Irish-Norwegian farm boy, rugged, gifted, argumentative, and persistent. By the time he was sixteen he had breezed through high school at Grand Rapids, Minnesota. After junior college he went to the University of Minnesota, picking up medals along the way and graduating with high honors. He was smart—at Corpus Christi he got a 4.0 grade on the first third of his navigation work, leading the whole class.

Danny was from Minnesota too. He was a little fighting Irishman, dark, wiry, full of sauce and afraid of nothing. Born on a farm, he was an expert horseman and a fine swimmer. When he and Casey were training at Wold-Chamberlain Field, Minneapolis (where they first met), Danny saved the lives of two boys who tired while swimming. A year later he jumped in the ocean at San Diego and saved a girl's life. This was all routine to Danny, for he had been lifeguard at the city pool in Marshall, Minnesota, for two seasons.

Both boys were original members of the eight-man flight that became known as the Flying Circus. When everyone was given a nickname for radio communication in the air, Casey was tagged "Fool" and Danny "Ish"—the Foolish Twins. They reveled in the name. In camp they were inseparable, and they always flew together. "I have to go along and look after Casey," Danny always said, ignoring the fact that Casey was more than able to take care of himself.

Baseball was Casey's great love, and it was from baseball that he got his strange, twisted grin. In his teens he played with the Grand Rapids, Minnesota, American Legion junior team. He rode home from one game through a cold wind, in the back end of a truck. Next morning when he got up there was no feeling in the right side of his face—it seemed to be frozen. Specialists later told him massage offered the only hope of recovering from this paralysis. When Casey read or studied, after that, he always rubbed his face.

His dad, Herman T. Brandon, was a veteran baseball player and saw that Casey got a good start at the game. They practiced in a stump-studded cow pasture on the farm, Brandon hitting long flies for his son to pull down. Casey learned to lay his ears back, run full tilt forty or fifty yards, turn around at exactly the right moment, and take in the ball. He had to be sure-footed to avoid the stumps.

When he was thirteen, he made his debut as center fielder in the Balsam Lake-Lawrence League in Northern Itasca

County. Nobody paid any attention to the little runt wandering around in the tall grass out there until a long fly was hit to center. Casey turned at the crack of the bat and caught the ball in deep center, spoiling a home run for somebody. The crowd came roaring to its feet. A few innings later the runt banged out a line drive to send in the winning run.

This performance made Casey a regular on the team. Later he organized a group of young players who gradually took over the Balsam Lake outfit. As second baseman and field general he led them to five consecutive League championships and permanent possession of the League trophy. Some seasons he hit as high as five hundred. Even among the fast Iron Range teams he was a prodigy—one of those rare players who consistently break up tight ball games. He knew the hitting characteristics of every man on the opposing teams, and was such a student of the game he could give the averages of almost any player in the major leagues any season within a few points. At the University of Minnesota he won his letter as regular center fielder.

When he worked or played, Casey put everything he had into it, and Danny was the same type. Maybe it was the Irish in them. Casey gave the credit to his dad. Competition in all games was of the ruthless, cutthroat variety at the Brandon farm, even at such innocuous pastimes as cribbage and horseshoes. No quarter was ever given or desired, but this code was emphasized: "If you lose after giving everything you've got, lose like a gentleman."

Casey was a Boy Scout and, like many farm youngsters, belonged to the 4-H Club. When his dad was ill with rheumatism, he ran the farm, passionately trying to make his field of potatoes the best in the United States, and every calf, pig or chicken on the farm a county fair champion.

Other boys liked to be with him, because he knew how to do things. Every week end he brought home friends who learned such diverse arts as the proper way to shovel manure or solve trigonometry problems. After working hard, they visited the swimming hole, then came back to play basketball near the barn, where an old ram waited patiently, ready to charge anyone who stooped down for a moment.

Casey had a big scrapbook filled with the awards he won in high school declamatory contests, programs of the plays he was in during high school and college days, 4-H Club prize ribbons, letters for basketball, baseball, and track, and pins won in debate and extemporaneous speech. He loved to argue and was unbeatable in history, foreign languages (French, German, Spanish and Italian), mathematics, spelling, and baseball statistics.

He was up in a plane only once before enlisting. But like most boys who turn into good fighter pilots, he had hunted since childhood. When he was eight years old, he trapped enough weasels and mink to buy a 16-gauge shotgun. With this he hunted ducks and partridges. When he was ten, a mining superintendent gave him a .33-caliber rifle. The next fall, aged eleven, Casey got his first deer. After that he was successful in bagging his deer each season. Once he ran two miles to get another rifle at home after his gun had jammed. He ran back, trailed a wounded deer through the brush, and put it out of its misery.

Illness at home delayed his education, but Casey was graduated *cum laude* from Minnesota in March, 1941. He went right into naval aviation and that's where he met

Danny, who was almost two years younger. Danny came up through the Marshall high school and the State Teachers' College at Mankato. He worked his way through, but found time for the CAA ground and flight course that led him into the Navy.

After preliminary training at Wold-Chamberlain—where they picked up Rog Haberman—Casey and Danny went to Jacksonville, Florida, then the naval air station at Corpus Christi, Texas. Boot Furlow joined them there. The Navy was choosy about its pilots in those days as it still is—in one day twelve out of sixteen men were washed out of one class at Corpus Christi. Once Cadet Brandon sent home a classic description of boot training:

Whenever an upperclassman knocks on our door, we shout "Ten-SHUN!" as loudly as possible and snap to an exaggerated posture, chest as far out as possible and stomach and rear as far in as possible. "Suck that gut in! Suck it in! Put some wrinkles in that chin! Wipe that smile off your face! Eyes on the bulkhead! O.K., mister, sound off!" And without moving a muscle I go "Aviation Cadet Brandon, Class 8-B, sir." They have you do it again and again until they're satisfied. Then they'll ask us what we're famous for, and if you're a flyer, you do some flying up and down the halls. If you're a schoolteacher, you get to lead a class. When they get through putting you through your paces, they shake hands and introduce themselves. Then they answer any questions you may have and give you all the low-down on what to expect. This is known as "getting the word" or "passing the word." It's all in fun and helps you a great deal more than it hurts you if you take it the right way. . . .

Casey and Danny waged a nip and tuck battle to see who would be first to get his wings. One day as the squadron prepared to solo in Vultees all planes were held up—there had been a crash. Number 65, flown by a man in the same class, had spun in from a thousand feet. The student miraculously escaped with deep cuts on his face, a slight concussion, and a broken collarbone. Danny and Casey had a queer feeling later as they looked down at the wrecked plane.

After getting their wings they were transferred, with Haberman and Furlow, to North Island, San Diego, then up the coast to Camp Kearney, whose beautifully modern 1898 tents were a good preparation for Guadalcanal. They were introduced to the 1,200 horsepower F4F Grumman Wildcat for the first time and went up to do formation loops, slow rolls, dive bombing and hedgehopping.

Casey was offered a chance to go to Annapolis to take an eighteen months' post-graduate course in aeronautical engineering, starting June 22. He turned it down. "It's a wonderful chance," he admitted, "but I'd get to fly only about four hours a month. There are other angles, too, such as the idea of sitting in a schoolroom while Danny and the boys are over there giving the Japs the business. I'll stick with the outfit. There are plenty of chair-sitting jobs to be had when I get too old to fly."

Meanwhile, Casey and Danny were carefully cultivating their reputation as prize screwballs. Always flying together, they put on a precision show when about to land—the planes were so close they seemed to be locked together. Once they were hedgehopping in a little valley. Doyle, ahead, flew down at a cow lying in the grass. She jumped up and he had to pull out quickly. Brandon laughed so hard he almost crashed into a near-by mountain.

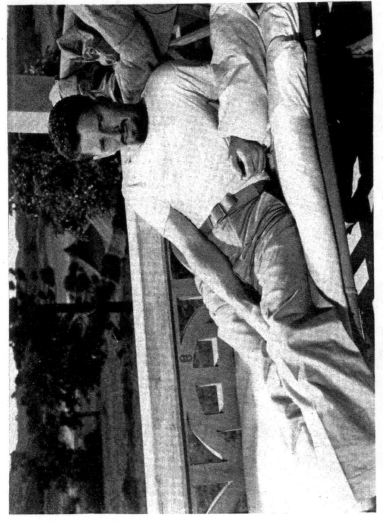

Recuperating in New Caledonia from a malaria attack, Joe shows his loss of weight from 195 to 160 pounds.

Here is Joe at Espiritu Santu, completely recovered from malaria, and on his way back to Guadalcanal.

Haberman and Furlow had a tent together. When they were on liberty, Casey and Danny "did a job" on the absentees' tent—nailing tables to the floor and pistol belts to the wall, rearranging the lighting system, mixing all clothing thoroughly, and once even providing a non-regulation back door.

On an oxygen hop, Casey passed out cold at 28,000 feet and didn't come out of it till he had reached about 5,000 feet. He hauled back on the stick, sat there groggily for about five minutes, then shook his head and flew back to the field. Only after landing did he realize what had happened. Part of his hood was blown off and one wing was kinked. When he told Major Davis about it, the Major commented with characteristic crispness, "Brother, you're living on velvet!"

Casey gave poker "lessons," sometimes collecting as much as ten dollars an evening in fees. When things were quiet, Doyle slept; once he dozed thirty hours out of forty-eight. His snoring was a problem that Casey solved by keeping a broom handle available. He wakened Danny by tapping him on the skull, then went to sleep hurriedly before his friend could regain unconsciousness. Danny regarded such things philosophically but did object in San Diego when Casey charged a $23.60 long distance call to his account at a hotel. The call was to Casey's fiancée, Peg O'Connell of St. Paul, Minnesota. "He squawked about it so much that I finally paid him the money," Casey later remarked with an injured expression. "It seems he doesn't value our friendship very much, worrying about such trifling sums of money."

Someone started the story back home that Doyle had been killed in the Midway battle. There were variations—he had crashed in the bay at San Diego, died in a midair crash at Honolulu, and drowned after taking off from a carrier. He got stacks of mail inquiring if the reports were true.

About this time I came in as executive officer of VMF 121. In an hour of dive-bombing practice, one of the boys hit the circle two out of five tries. Doyle showed him up by getting three for five; then Casey came along and rang the gong with five straight hits.

One day we went down to North Island to see a Zero which had been shot down in Alaska. We all stood there in the hangar and had a long, sober look at the thing.

Weeks later and thousands of miles from San Diego, after leaving New Caledonia on the little aircraft carrier whose name is a secret, Casey wrote a thoughtful letter to his folks. When I saw it long afterward, I thought it was one of the finest things I had ever read. I still think so.

There is no way of predicting how things will go from here on, but you can be certain it will be lots of fun and plenty exciting. This war has changed my life a thousandfold, and I am happier beyond belief as a result. You will remember very well, no doubt, that I always did care more for play than work, and all this flying is just like a game to me, only the stakes are a little higher. It seems rather ridiculous for us to be wanting to jump in and get our fool heads shot off, but every man in the outfit wants to get in there and get it over with, one way or another. This business of going out into action is the most exciting thing I've ever run across in my life, although we know we are not all coming back. I would like to come back because I know that Peg and all of you will be waiting for my return. But if I do not come back, it will happen so fast that I will never realize it. This is my life from now on, dear people; it travels fast while it lasts and ends equally as fast. That is the main reason I am not afraid to go out;

I'll be gloriously happy until it happens and then the end will come so quickly I won't have time to be unhappy or even frightened. However, it is only the nice kids who get the axe, so my kind is bound to be around when it is all over.

But let's get back to Guadalcanal, where this story really belongs. On the night of October 13, at the height of the worst shelling the island ever got, Danny, Casey, Furlow, and Haberman were crowded in a foxhole. After two and a half hours of it, a near-by oil dump was shooting flames two hundred feet high, ammunition dumps were going off, planes were blazing around the field, and flares were hanging in the sky like an evening at the planetarium.

"Say," Danny inquired during a lull, "do you think it would reveal our position if I lit a cigarette?"

Danny was enchanted by the coconuts on Guadalcanal. "When I was a boy," he said, "Mother always had to hide the coconut from me so I wouldn't eat it all. Here we're camped right in the middle of a coconut grove, and I can have all I want."

He had great contempt for Japanese marksmanship. "Those goonies couldn't hit the broad side of a barn," he often remarked.

One day Danny's plane needed repairs and he couldn't go up. It was the first time he hadn't flown with Casey. That night we waited uncomfortably for a plane that hadn't come back. It was Casey's.

I don't like to think of the expression on Danny's face. He quit his wisecracking abruptly and became grim and quiet. By that time he had official credit for five planes shot down. "Those goonies are going to pay if it's the last thing I do," he said bitterly. "I'm going to double my score for Casey."

One day Danny himself turned up missing. A flight mate told of seeing a Grumman chasing a Zero right into the sea. That was three weeks after Casey went down.

Danny, who had sworn to avenge his friend's death, must have been overtrying that day. We missed those two boys. Thinking later of their short and tragic history, the high promise and the glory of their youth, we fought more savagely against the enemy.

A date I remember among that strange welter of days on Guadalcanal is November 9. I got up early and went down to headquarters command post to be awarded the Distinguished Flying Cross by Admiral W. F. Halsey, Jr., naval commander in the South Pacific.

The day was very quiet and the ceremony very short. Three of us got the DFC that day—Big Bill Freeman, a member of my flight, and Lieutenant Wallace Wethe, a member of our squadron. We lined up in the shade of the jungle trees, and the only disturbance was some cameramen. Admiral Halsey gave a short talk—only a few sentences.

We went down there in our flight suits so we would be able to go right back and take off as soon as we got through.

My citation read:

For extraordinary achievement while participating in aerial flights with Marine Fighting Squadron 121 in the Solomon Islands area. During the period Oct. 13 to Oct. 20, 1942, inclusive, Captain Foss shot down six enemy Zero fighters and one enemy bomber in aerial combat. His constant aggressiveness, skill, and leadership during these engagements were worthy of the highest traditions of the Naval Service.

Everything there could have been said as well of the other boys in the Flying Circus.

Admiral Halsey, who was placed in command of our area October 24, told a good story on himself that trip. At lunch with General Vandegrift and other officers he had been pleased with the food. "This," he said, "is the best utilization of materials I have found in the entire southwest Pacific. I'm going to make it a point to personally commend the mess sergeant."

So the Admiral and other officers went back to the kitchen. They found the Sergeant, a tough, hard-bitten veteran. The Admiral gave a little informal speech. It embarrassed the Sergeant to death. He blushed, averted his head coyly, and rolled his hands into his apron.

"Aw, horsemeat, Admiral, horsemeat," he blurted finally. (This is not an exact quotation.)

We flew patrol that day but ran into no excitement. Lieutenant John B. Maas, Jr., twenty-two, of Grosse Point, Michigan, a nephew of Colonel Melvin Maas, the flying congressman from Minnesota, came back O.K. He had been missing since the night of the seventh.

Next day I took some new pilots on an indoctrination tour of the islands. With me I took a gunny sack filled with cigarettes, chewing and smoking tobacco, razor blades, and some of the newest magazines (three months old). I threw the sack out at the mission where I had stayed.

Other pilots who landed at the same island later were reminded that Foss had dropped a little remembrance and it might be well if they did the same.

In a few days another missing man came back—Lieutenant Jack Stub of Minneapolis. On the day I had my experience in the sea I had seen a Grumman with motor trouble, chugging along slowly. Lieutenant Stub turned out to be the pilot. He was later shot down and also spent some time on Malaita. Stub is the only son of Dr. J. A. O. Stub, pastor emeritus of Central Lutheran Church in Minneapolis, and during World War I the director of all war work done by the Lutheran synods of America.

We learned that the Malaita grapevine which had brought news of the eradication of a Jap camp a hundred miles away was remarkably accurate. Such an attack was actually made by a forty-man Marine squad led by Lieutenant James Crain, of Ada, Oklahoma. Rowing to the island in two native boats, the raiders cut their way through the jungle and surrounded the Jap outpost, which had a wireless station.

While the Japs were at breakfast in their mess hall, the Marines let them have it. Out of twenty-two men only one got away. He was badly wounded, and a doctor said he could not live. Another Jap was brought home a prisoner. The raiders returned with the enemy wireless set and a boatload of captured weapons.

Armistice Day failed to live up to its name. At five-thirty in the morning we flew to Rekata Bay and made a strafing attack. Anti-aircraft fire was not apparent. All our planes returned.

The Japanese were putting in everything they had. Later in the day we were attacked by two waves of bombers. The first consisted of ten bombers, escorted by twelve fighters in an attack on ships unloading men and supplies. Not a ship was hit, and our boys got six bombers and five fighters out of this wave.

The second wave had twenty-five bombers and five fighters, of which we got only five bombers and a Zero. In all the boys knocked down seven big bombers, four dive bombers, and six Zeros.

Boot and I had gone out in search of a four-motor flying boat which saw us coming and managed to escape in the clouds. We returned to the field to gas, so got off too late for any action when the bombers appeared. We climbed out of range of the bombs but were unable to get into position to make any run. We had to watch the other boys perform and keep score for them.

We saw Rog Haberman chase a smoking bomber all the way down. When he landed, he had to go to the hospital to have shrapnel removed from a leg. He was so excited, nevertheless, that he was jumping up and down. "When I tried to nail that bomber," he said, "I went under the wing. I looked over and saw the two Jap pilots, one sitting behind the other. They looked at me, and their eyes were as big as coconuts."

Lieutenant David K. Allen, twenty-three, of Wichita, Kansas, shot down a Zero with a diving run over Savo Island, then was caught, too low for maneuvering, when a second Zero hopped his tail. His plane was shot into the sea, but he managed to bail out at eight hundred feet. He was caught on the tail for an instant but fought free and landed in the water. He was picked up immediately by a boat and returned to the field. (Lieutenant Allen was killed in a crash in line of duty April 14, 1943, in the South Pacific area.)

Our squadron leader, Major Davis, came back wounded.

A shell exploded in his cockpit and put buckshot marks all over his face, but he was ready to fly again in a couple of days.

There was worse news. In that fight we lost Sergeant Palko, the "Fighting Hunky" of Hazleton, Pennsylvania; Lieutenant Joseph L. Narr, of Hickman Mills, Missouri; Lieutenant Roy M. A. Ruddell, of Newcastle, Indiana, and Lieutenant Simpson, of Chicago. We also lost Lieutenant T. H. Mann, Jr., of Terre Haute, Indiana, but he later returned.

We learned that Sergeant Palko had a midair crash and fell off the shore of Tulagi. Lieutenant Mann, who landed at Tulagi, was present at his funeral there.

CHAPTER XII

Y

THAT NIGHT A HEAVY AMERICAN TASK FORCE CREPT UP TO THE
island, west of our land positions. At the crack of dawn it
plastered the Japs with a heavy bombardment which continued pleasantly for hours. The only effective enemy answer
was a five-inch shell which killed five sailors on the destroyer *Buchanan* and slightly damaged the ship itself.

They were still pouring shells into the Japs at two-fifteen
when fighter-escorted enemy torpedo bombers launched an
attack. We knew the planes were coming but did not know
exactly from where. We were circling at twenty-nine thousand feet, orbiting high above the harbor.

Over Florida Island hung a cloud at about twenty thousand feet. I called the boys and suggested that probably the
enemy planes were over that bank. Not daring to go down
low for fear they might come in the other way, we circled
over the bank, waiting for them to come out.

Finally we sighted them far below, breaking out of clouds,
at about five hundred feet. It was a mass attack from a fast-

121

moving group of thirty-one planes which had been under the cloud bank and had peeled off to dive from there. They were going about three hundred knots, fifty feet or less above the water, off the east point of Florida Island.

"Let's go, gang!" I said, and dove full throttle. We went down so fast our cold planes frosted over and we had a tough time seeing out—had to claw the frost off the inside of the windshields. The cockpit hood of my plane burst and pads at the edge of the fuselage blew off. We hit the Japs from behind and started picking them off, before they could make their runs. Major Paul Fontana's flight and eight P-39s soon joined us.

I pulled up within one hundred yards of the nearest bomber and gave him a burst. His right motor caught fire. He was only twenty-five or fifty feet above the water and as soon as the flames broke out, the pilot sat down in the channel. As he let down, the right wing hit the water first, and the plane did a cartwheel right there.

I looked on all sides and saw bombers burning in the same fashion as mine had. The sky was black with anti-aircraft fire from our warships.

As I passed the ships, a Zero came diving from somewhere and made a run on me. He chose an annoying time, for I had a bomber up front and was just ready to shoot. I had to haul up and give a short burst, which happened to be dead on the Zero. He blew up practically on the water.

At once I switched my attention back to the bomber. I had to come in carefully at an angle, out of range of his stingers. My first shots missed because I was looking around for enemy planes that could be expected any second. I crossed to the other side and gave him a short burst which hit the left side of the plane right at the base of the wing.

Fire at once started, spreading to the left motor. The pilot put the fire out with a perfect landing on the water. I went over as the plane hit, and the turret gunner shot at me.

I pulled off and started after another bomber. I hit him a few times, but my bullets struck far outside his motor, and didn't start any fire or do any apparent damage.

Just as I was getting set for a better shot, two Zeros arrived bearing gifts for me. I got down almost on the water and started toward Savo Island, a near-by little hunk of ground we owned. I skidded back and forth on the water, trying to avoid Zero bullets.

An army P-39 cut in front of me and made a run on the bomber. At once the Zeros started after the P-39 and the bomber disappeared in the clouds with the P-39 on his tail. Our man finally got the bomber and escaped his pursuers.

The reason I had suddenly become unsociable was that I was out of ammunition. I was also on my reserve tank of gas, so did not have very long. I climbed into a cloud hanging on the mountain back of Savo and circled around, sticking my head out to look for Zeros. Once I started for home, but a Zero came and gave me a good run. I turned back into the cloud and climbed for altitude.

Just before I dove, here came a loaded Jap bomber, circling the island. I got on the radio and begged somebody to come get him. He was all alone and could have been had for the asking.

But everyone was engaged in dogfights high overhead. I dove out of the cloud and headed for home. Between Savo and Henderson Field I counted twelve Jap bombers floating in the water, several of them with crew members standing on the wings.

A few torpedoes were released but no hits were scored on our shipping. Of the thirty-one fighters and bombers, thirty were shot down, nine by AA fire from the ships. We got the rest. Only that one bomber escaped.

I did expect to see one of our warships missing. After I had shot down my first plane, I saw at the right a flaming Jap craft flying right into the side of the 9,950 ton heavy cruiser, *San Francisco*. The pilot had been hit and lost control of the plane. It seemed that he blew up the entire ship, but apparently it was only his gasoline exploding. There was little damage. Thirty men were killed, however.

Lieutenant Nehf was back that day, his first time out since he sustained an eye injury. Art, a rough and ready boy who cuts his hair short, was hot as a two-dollar pistol. He shot down three planes. I saw him get one. It was a beautiful technical job.

My three planes that day were credited as Numbers twenty, twenty-one and twenty-two for me.

A big naval battle raged in the vicinity that night. It was close enough so we could hear the reports of the big explosions and see the flickering flashes, which often lighted the entire horizon.

On the island, where the outcome of the battle mattered most, we saw only the flashes, flaring like great northern lights, and heard the growling of the guns. Scuttlebutt next morning brought us the news that the enemy had taken a beating, but we had suffered losses as well. The *San Francisco* had been hit and important senior officers killed, among them Rear Admiral Daniel J. Callaghan and Captain Cassin Young. Several of our destroyers were also put out of action.

I took off at dawn on a scout mission. On the other side of Savo Island we located a Jap battleship moving slowly through the water, accompanied by a cruiser and five destroyers. On the near side of Savo, in the channel, two of our destroyers were burning and deserted.

We started working on the cruiser and battleship. In the afternoon we escorted a torpedo and dive bomber attack on the battle wagon, which had a superstructure like a pagoda and seemed to be of the old *Kongo* class. I came down in a steep attack, strafing the cruiser, then pulled out and headed for the battleship, with my boys close behind.

As I was two hundred yards away, about fifty feet above the water, a torpedo dropped by Captain George Dooley, twenty-four, of Hopeland, California, scored a direct hit amidships. The colors of the explosion, which shot water, steam, fire, and debris high in the air, were wonderful.

I passed within a few feet of the superstructure and made a sharp turn to the right. I had intended to turn left but changed my mind. A moment later an anti-aircraft shell burst where I would have been had I turned left. I looked back and saw the battleship's big guns still shooting into the water, sending up great geysers fifty to seventy-five feet high as a defense against our torpedo planes. All of our boys returned safely from that trip. In the morning other flights shot down about a dozen Zeros.

Later that day the battleship was sunk. I didn't go out on this attack, though. Just before a big rainstorm started and closed in the ships, we saw personnel being transferred to destroyers. When the storm lifted, the battleship was gone and the water was covered with oil. I went out and strafed the destroyers again.

There's a little footnote on Captain Dooley that shouldn't be omitted. Seeing him for the first time, you observe scars on his face. Later you notice one of his little fingers is stiff. That's where the story comes in.

When he was a cadet in elementary flying formation at Pensacola, one of his wingmen was crossing over on a flight. Misjudging distance, he got too close and chopped into Dooley's gas tank with his prop. The gas ignited and gushed back into the cockpit like a flood of liquid fire.

Dooley got out of there somehow and fell like a torch toward the earth. He let himself go for a long time, as long as possible, hoping this would put the fire out. But he was still blazing when at last he pulled the cord. Then, of course, the flames went up into the chute.

He got a pretty hard bump when he struck, but was able to roll over and put the fire out. When they picked him up, all the meat was burned from his face, his eyes were injured, the cartilage was burned from his nose, and his hands were almost charred. They wrote him off as a flyer right there.

But Dooley only wanted to do one thing and that was to fly a Marine plane. He underwent operation after operation to get the use of his fingers back. Every time he flunked a physical exam, he went back for some more surgery. This went on for about a year.

Sheer determination seemed to bring him around. His eyes came back, and his hands got pretty good again. The doctors, still said it was no dice, though; the skin on his hands was so delicate that even a slight bruise was a serious matter.

But Dooley couldn't be argued down. "I want to fly," he told them, over and over, with his chin stuck out. Finally they gave him a chance. I guess it was more a tribute to his guts than anything else. Anyway, he finished a year behind his class and became a great fighting man—one of the very best.

The night was a bearcat—more tough shelling offshore. At daylight we took off up the channel on an escort mission. At the lower tip of New Georgia Island I saw the smoke of a burning cruiser and destroyer that had been disabled by our dive bombers.

Shortly after noon word was received that fourteen Jap transports and cargo ships were coming down the channel, escorted by warships. On the first attack by our planes all the warships turned and fled, leaving the others to shift for themselves. The first wave of bombers and torpedo planes set fire to several and sank another outright.

My outfit was sent to escort dive bombers and torpedo planes again. Colonel Bauer accompanied us. "I'm not going to let you fellows have all the fun," he said.

The Coach, Boot Furlow, and I circled for some time to provide air cover while the attack proceeded on warships and transports up the channel. Finally the Colonel and Boot dove steeply to strafe a transport to my left, so steeply I lost sight of them. I took another to the right.

I came down to 3,000 feet, started shooting and continued down to almost mast height, riddling the decks, which had thousands of our little friends congregated on them. We really killed a slew of them that day.

Then we went tearing for home, right on the water. Tracers started coming over my shoulder. I turned and saw two Zeros coming toward us. The Coach turned and went head on at one. Both planes were firing. Suddenly the Zero blew into a million pieces.

Boot and I went after the other. Trying unsuccessfully to catch it, we flew directly over a Jap destroyer, which cut loose at us with anti-aircraft.

We turned back to get the Colonel and go home. When we reached the spot where pieces of the Zero were floating, we couldn't find Colonel Bauer. I spotted an oil slick about two miles away. Just outside the slick we found the Colonel, swimming.

I circled a second time, a few feet off the water, and tried to drop him my rubber boat but it would not come out. He jumped up out of the water, waved, and pointed toward home. Boot and I tried to radio in but could not get our call through. We went home full throttle to get a rescue plane.

Major Joe Renner, thirty, of Bowbells, North Dakota, and I took off to pick up the Colonel. By now it was pitch black and all we could see were five enemy ships ablaze under low hanging clouds. These ships must have contained oil or ammunition, for occasional great explosions practically blew the roof out of the sky.

After circling vainly for some time, we returned to the field.

The next morning the entire flight took off before daylight to resume the search. Four cargo ships—the only ones that had not been set afire the day before—were rounding Cape Esperance. We sent word back to the field by radio and

At home, Joe's widowed mother, Mrs. Mary Foss, waited patiently and proudly for letters from her son. The Foss home has no electricity; the letters were read by lamplight. This one promised her that he would be home soon.

(Chicago Tribune photo)

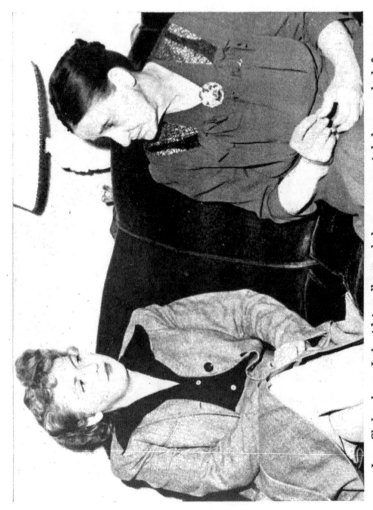

June Shakstad was Joe's girl in college and they were married three weeks before he went overseas. Here wife and mother are pictured as news came that Joe had shot down his twenty-sixth Jap plane, to equal Eddie Rickenbacker's First World War record.

(Acme)

continued on our way. Farther up the line, one of the burning ships had sunk and the others were still blazing. Two Jap reconnaissance planes appeared. Seven of the boys went after one and left the other for me. I made a pass at him, and his rear gunner fired on me. On the first shot I hit him. When he started to smoke, I decided he would go down and started after the plane the others were chasing. Just then it blew up, spraying the sky with debris.

Looking back, I saw my Jap was still going. As I went back to finish him, he made a sharp bank directly in front of me. It was a long shot—about three hundred yards—but he and my bullets got there at the same time. Smack in the center of the plane flames came out. He pushed over and disappeared. The rear gunner was still shooting as the plane hit the water.

We searched every inch of the area for the Colonel but found nothing except some empty Jap lifeboats still floating.

When we returned, three of the four cargo ships we had seen earlier off the cape were ablaze at Tassafaronga, from our dive bombers. We strafed the fourth and also sprinkled the beach, so that anybody who was interested in getting any of the cargo would be out of luck. Right then a dive bomber laid one in the hold of the undamaged ship and started a good fire. The four ships burned and exploded the rest of the day. If anyone wishes to see them, they are still there on the beach at Guadalcanal.

We figured at least 20,000 Japs died in the eight transports which were sunk out of that convoy. Hundreds of those lads were seen for a time struggling in the sea. The ships were believed to have carried three divisions of troops with full equipment.

That morning I was sick when I took off. I felt lousy and could not have made that last flight except for the excitement, which built me up so I felt pretty good. When we got back to the field, I was hardly able to sit up.

It was malaria. I ached all over, had a fever of 103½°, and was so sick I thought I was going to die. I imagined I saw and heard airplanes, my head buzzed, my eyes were swollen, and I could not see very well. They gave me quinine.

Next day, which was rainy with no activity, Bill Marontate took over my flight. I had a fever of 103° and was very ill. Everyone was down in the mouth because of the loss of the Colonel. Besides being a good boss to work for and a fine tactician, he was a fighter pilot of consummate skill. In the only four flights in which he contacted the enemy, he shot down one big bomber, four dive bombers, and six Zeros.

News of the results from four straight nights of naval battles offshore filtered in slowly. Our boys, with battleships in major action for the first time since the Spanish-American War, had decisively beaten a numerically superior enemy fleet. In the hit-and-run fighting of those thundering nights and days the Japs lost two battleships, eight cruisers, six destroyers, eight troopships, and four cargo ships. Once during the confusion two separate enemy forces engaged each other. Our losses were two light cruisers and seven destroyers in all.

The Army went up to Bougainville, hit a ship, and shot down three Zeros.

On November 19 I left Guadalcanal in a DC-3 with Boot

Furlow, Grow, Bate, and Big Bill Freeman, who was sick almost to the point of death. Marontate, Loesch, and Mann had gone on before.

In a few hours we were at a cool island far away. I still felt terrible. I went to bed and stayed.

CHAPTER XIII

Υ

THE ISLAND WAS NEW CALEDONIA. WE WERE GIVEN BEDS IN AN old French doctor's home—much better than a tent—and warned we would have to be inactive quite a while. Ben Finney was in the next bed, with malaria too.

I was given forty-five grains of quinine the first five days. Then the dose tapered to fifteen grains and finally to five every other day. On top of the malaria I had dysentery. My weight dropped from 197 pounds to 160, and I looked like a walking boneyard. My eyes were sunk in and there were big black circles under them.

The boys went hunting deer, but I was still too sick to go. They brought back one carcass, which we had for dinner next day. It was very good. We saw and enjoyed several motion pictures—*Jesse James* was one. They all seemed wonderful.

The rest of the time we just loafed around, reflecting that the Japs were just as eligible for malaria as we were and

132

probably suffered as much. Haberman was the only man in my flight who didn't get it, in spite of all precautions. Bill Freeman was so sick for a while he couldn't even talk.

The town of Noumea is a foreign-looking French settlement, crowded and dirty. It was almost impossible to buy anything except at Army and Navy post exchanges. The town was jammed with soldiers of all kinds, including French Negroes in short pants.

On November 30, feeling better, we flew in a few hours to Sydney, Australia, right in the middle of the east coast. The first thing we did was take a good hot bath to soak out some of the dirt. It was our first hot bath since leaving the United States in August. Next I cut off my beard and shaved. When I walked up and stood in a circle where Major Harold (Soupy) Campbell, Middlesex, Vermont, and some others were talking, they didn't even recognize me.

We had some big steaks. During our stay in Sydney we had steaks three times a day.

It felt odd to be in civilization again. Sydney resembles the States except that automobiles drive on the wrong side of the street. Australians thought I talked with a funny brogue and tried to guess whether I was from the South or Midwest. I was always puzzling somebody.

Loafing around there and enjoying the good eats, I met many people I knew. One was Bob Cromie, a correspondent I like because he is a regular fellow and always quoted me accurately. I met "Killer" Caldwell, the Australian ace who shot down twenty Germans and Italians over the desert, and "Bluey" Truscott, their second-ranking ace, who got fifteen Germans over the Channel. Caldwell and I talked about shooting men in chutes—something I never did because I felt it jeopardized me and I could be more profitably employed somewhere else.

I played poker all one night, was invited to tea by hospitable Australians, and visited Bondi Beach with Ben Finney. On December 7, the anniversary of Pearl Harbor, I thought of all the blood that had flowed under the bridge since then and wished my boys who had died were with me to enjoy the rest they had worked for. The day that Pearl Harbor was attacked, I was officer of the day at Saufley Field, Pensacola.

I ran into an old friend—Colonel Burnette—and found he had been betting on me all the time. When we left the United States, he bet I would get the largest number of planes in the squadron. He was still chuckling over his winnings.

The boys ribbed me considerably about an interview that appeared in one of the papers. Another flyer had kiddingly said, "Smoke was a-pourin', the rivets were a-poppin', and then the wings fell off. But the old ship made it." When the story came out, the remark was credited to me. The boys called me "the only man in the world who ever landed a ship without wings." It was too much of a compliment.

One day I had a relapse and felt like dying; shortly afterward I felt like two million dollars. Caldwell took me to an airdrome and I gave a talk to the air squadrons. "When you find yourself all alone out there," I said at one point, "head for home."

One of the RAAF pilots asked if that were "quite the sporting thing to do, old boy?" I answered: "Look, when

I was all alone, I scooted for home. I'm still around. The guys that fought by themselves are dead."

Those were blunt words but valuable for an airman to remember.

I will never forget how well people treated us in Sydney, and what a good time we had there. I even got in a little flying—a pleasant and instructive hour and a half in a Spitfire.

One of the old friends I met was Thomas Fortune Ryan, who left the presidency of Mid-Continent Airlines to be a major in the Army air forces. We spent hours talking about people we knew.

On December 16 we returned to New Caledonia, where I found three letters from my wife and a Christmas present— a knitted sweater—from my sister, Flora Mary. A physical checkup showed me to be in 4.0 condition.

I met another friend—Lieutenant Bob Sorenson of Chicago, a naval flyer and an old cadet roommate. One day Bill Freeman and I visited the ships in the harbor to test out their food. Another time we had a French supper in a café—about twenty courses, served a dab at a time.

On December 23 everyone started north except me. I had a positive malaria smear. Christmas Day found me a dinner guest at a French doctor's home. We had chicken, turkey, dressing, potatoes and gravy, fruitcake, and many other things. I couldn't understand a word the family said, but they just sat there eating and laughing and laughing, and I followed their example. Two days later I went north to another island and rejoined some of the boys.

On the thirty-first I received orders to return to Guadalcanal, and got everything ready. I took off with Loesch and Freeman, feeling that one good air fight would restore me to perfect condition.

We spent all night flying and arrived at Henderson Field in the morning.

CHAPTER XIV

Υ

WE WENT AT ONCE TO THE FIGHTER STRIP. EVERYTHING HAD changed in the six weeks we had been away. There was now a field with a steel mat runway instead of the old cow pasture. We had M. P.'s, telephones, good roads, moving pictures—and no excitement. The field had not been bombed since December 14, and there hadn't been a multiple bombing attack since we left.

Lieutenant Colonel Sam Jack was the new fighter commander. The flight roster for our second trip included, besides myself, Bill Marontate, Greg Loesch, old Rog Haberman, Big Bill Freeman, Oscar Bate, Boot Furlow, and a newcomer to my flight, Lieutenant Frank (Skeezix) Presley, twenty-two, of Encinitas, California, a quiet, reserved, and bashful youngster, but a courageous fighter and a good man to have on our side.

Five men who were original members of the flight or had been with it at one time or another were gone—Danny

137

Doyle, Casey Brandon, Joe Palko, Andy Andrews, and Gene Nuwer.

There was little sleep to be had the first night back. Our new camp was only fifty feet from the big artillery, which fired continuously all night. Next day we moved to a new spot on a high hill, where we had two tents, a sea breeze, and a view of the water. Back of the tents was a steep cliff. The only drawback was that here artillery shells whistled over our heads.

On our second night Jap bombers came over and dropped a load, but we never even woke up. By this time we had decided if bombs were going to hit us, they would do it anyway—so why get up? We had the dawn patrol hop and later spent some time chewing the rag with the Army boys. They are fine fellows and by this time had made a brilliant record. In the shower at the powerhouse we met Captain Herman (Hap) Hanson, Kansas City, Missouri, an old buddy who was best man at my wedding.

Two Grummans failed to return due to a storm. Next morning, after a night during which some greenhorn sounded the alert several times thinking we were being attacked, Greg Loesch and three of the boys ran into dive bombers with satisfying results. Greg got two, Freeman two, Presley one, and Lieutenant Jack B. Gifford, age twenty-three, Shaker Heights, Ohio, substituting for Bate, one. Two army P-38s were shot down.

It wasn't a bad start for a new flight. The bombers were shot down over one of the islands to the north. Even more gratifying was the aftermath of this fight. On the way home our men, out of ammunition, were jumped by a dozen Zeros. Yet they bluffed the Zeros for miles by having the two wingmen turn menacingly toward the enemy whenever a Zero tried to make a run. It was smart maneuvering. The Zeros finally turned back without knowing that none of the Wildcats could have fired a shot. Curiously enough, one of the Zeros caught fire and fell into the sea off Cape Esperance.

Tired of walking about the island, I borrowed a threeton truck from Major Bob Denig, Jr., thirty-three, of Richmond, Virginia, son of Brigadier General Denig, head of Marine public relations. He mentioned something about brakes, but it failed to register with me. Greg Loesch and I went for a ride.

We climbed a steep hill which had a curve near the top. At the summit we stopped. I threw the truck out of gear and put on the brakes. A catastrophe followed. Down the hill like a greased pig in a chute we went. There wasn't a sign of brakes on that truck. When we reached the curve, we were going much too fast to turn. We took off on a straight course. Directly on our route all the telephone wires on Guadalcanal were strung, sagging down low, between forty-five and fifty of them. We went through them like nothing.

Next we went through a big ammunition dump, where tons of ammunition were laid in holes. We didn't hit a hole. Finally we coasted to a stop. Greg got out and untangled the wire which had draped itself over the cab. Then we left there.

We used to kid each other to pass away the time. One night Jap planes were flying over and our anti-aircraft was roaring. "It's dangerous to stand outside," we told some of the boys. "The pieces of anti-aircraft might fall down and knock a hole in your head and kill you."

Rog Haberman started a game. He got some rocks and threw them in the air so they landed close. Loesch and Presley dove under a truck. We kept them there too. Every time rocks hit close to the truck, they yelled, "God, there goes another one!"

Another time Presley was scouting around and Boot was in the sack. Presley made a noise like a bomb, threw a rock, and hit the side of the tent a wallop with his hand. Boot nearly broke his neck getting to a foxhole. He thought he was gone sure.

One night there was a light raid. We awoke and heard some of the new fellows running. "Where is a foxhole? Where is a foxhole?" one yelled. "I don't know," screamed another. "Just jump in any old hole, whether it's a head or not." (A "head" is the Navy equivalent of the Army's latrine.)

I used to amuse the boys by imitating a Jap general calling the roll after we'd shot down an entire squadron of his planes. I had names for all the missing men.

A night bombing was the first in weeks. Five bombs dropped by a single plane killed one man and injured several others.

Even so, the hovering canopy of danger which had hung over the island in October and November was gone. Guarded by warships and aircraft, our transports landed reinforcements while the Navy bombarded the new Jap airfield at Munda, 180 miles away, to keep enemy planes on the ground. The Japs were now resorting to submarines to supply their troops. We ruled the air completely.

Days of the "Tokyo Express"—a force of one cruiser and four destroyers which landed nine hundred men on the island nightly—were over. Submarines landed the barest necessities by night—oil drums and small rafts loaded with food. We patrolled the shore line every morning to shoot up as much of these supplies as possible.

Food was landed, too, by parachute from flying boats. These iron rations consisted of dry rice, dried soy bean sauce, and a kind of hardtack. That was all, but the Japs continued healthy.

One day we found a Jap schooner, with a radio station aboard, camouflaged against a cliff with a net over it. In order to attack we had to come directly toward the bluff, taking the tops off the trees a moment later.

We riddled the schooner at the water line and returned to the field just as darkness fell. Next day only a mast was sticking out of the water.

While patrolling, we spotted two Jap breakfast fires and strafed them, ruining someone's morning tea, possibly. After reloading we accompanied bombers to Munda, where hits were scored on the field. There was plenty of anti-aircraft, but it got no hits. Jap planes remained in the distance, too timid to argue with us.

Something went wrong with Loesch's landing gear—one wheel was up and one was down. If he had landed on the field, the single wheel would have probably pitched him over and killed him. He decided to make a crash landing in the ocean just off the field. He hit terribly hard but got out all right with a cut on the forehead.

Little things made up our days in early January. I suddenly noticed that all of my boys snored and was amused when they all indignantly denied it. Major Campbell and his squadron arrived from the south. Our artillery was continually firing. That zoot suit article in *Collier's* really got the boys talking. What they said would blister this paper.

Japs at night cut loose two barges containing rice, fuel, and ammunition, between Savo Island and Cape Esperance. As the barges floated toward Jap-held territory, our planes strafed and set them afire. None of them got in.

Outfits led by Major Campbell and Captain Hunter Reinburg, twenty-four, of Los Angeles, tangled with sixteen Zeros up the channel, shooting down several with the loss of one of our boys.

Boot and I spotted Jap troops sneaking along the shore road, heading for the front. I called to Boot on the radio and said, "I'm going to do a wingover, and when I start shooting, you start shooting right under my wing."

So we cut loose at them. Later we circled back and saw dozens of them kicking in the road. Even those who hid behind palm trees got it, for our .50-caliber machine gun slugs go through palm trees like a knife through butter.

A few moments later a machine gunner fired on me from a ridge. I shut this bird off with one pass.

Hap Hanson came back after a little adventure. His reconnaissance plane was hit and set afire. He had to sideslip into the ocean back of the Jap lines, getting a cut on the head. Then he had to do a swimming job around the front lines to get back. He had my mail in his pocket when he made the swim. When he got in, he was taken to a first aid station, fixed up, and given dry clothes to wear.

But some dirty rat stole his clothes and got my mail. I would rather have lost a thousand dollars, so scarce was mail on Guadalcanal.

Hap always called me Pop, and I called him Son. He

was only twenty-three but had been in the Marines a year longer than I had.

It was a memorable treat when Lieutenant Bill Wilson, forty-nine, of Atlanta, Georgia, brought over three apple pies. They didn't last long. Pies brought as high as eleven dollars apiece during the Guadalcanal campaign.

We went up the line again on an escort looking for destroyers which we didn't find. On the way home the bombers unloaded on Munda Airfield. There was no air opposition but a lot of anti-aircraft.

I had to take over as operations officer—a thankless job. Phones rang continually. I thought of the old days, when we had only one telephone, which was out of commission most of the time because of trucks running over the wire. If anybody thought his business was important enough, he came to see us personally.

Jap planes came over after dark and bombed the field. It was the first multiple plane attack since November. We stood on a hilltop and watched the raid, which cost us the lives of six mechanics. Jap destroyers later approached Savo and our PT boats took them on. Jap troops by this time were crowded on the northern hump of the island. Their time was growing short.

On the morning of January 15 I was up at dawn to take over operations duty. The day opened with an attack by one of our Catalina planes on five Japanese destroyers sixteen miles northeast of the Russell Islands, sixty miles northwest of Guadalcanal. The Catalina got one sure hit and two near misses on one destroyer.

Later a force of Dauntless dive bombers, escorted by Wildcats and Airacobras, located nine enemy destroyers 140 miles northwest of Lunga Point and hit two of them. When Zeros attempted to intercept, Captain Reinburg's flight shot down eleven, losing four of our pilots. Major Tom Pierce, Coronado, California, got three Zeros but was wounded and had to bail out of his plane. He was picked up by one of our destroyers.

The day was beginning to warm up and look like old times. One of our planes on patrol near the island engaged and shot down three Zeros.

The Army boys, in Flying Fortresses, Lightnings, Airacobras, and Warhawks, went out on another attack. Their objective was five Jap destroyers thirty-seven miles southeast of Fasi Island, in the Shortland Island area, three hundred miles from Guadalcanal. No hits were scored on the destroyers, but twelve enemy biplanes were shot down. None of our planes was lost.

Then came the afternoon.

My outfit escorted dive bombers which had been assigned to attack an enemy transport and destroyer up the line a ways. Before we reached the target, Captain Loesch was forced to return to Henderson Field because of engine trouble, leaving seven planes in my flight. We were accompanied, however, by several Army P-39s.

As we neared the ships, the P-39s were attacked by a swarm of new square-wing Zeros, supposed to have added speed and climbing ability. Three of my boys, led by Bill Marontate, went down to get in on the fun. I remained at altitude because several Zeros were circling there also.

In short order there were several Jap chutes in the air. I saw one Wildcat too, its left wing missing, spinning slowly

toward the water at about a 45° angle. This was apparently
Lieutenant Marontate.

The fight moved upward. I fired one short burst at a Zero
but didn't get a hit. He dove to a lower altitude and I let him
go. Then in the distance I noticed a Grumman, piloted by
Oscar Bate, coming my way, surrounded by Zeros that
seemed to be sparring for a favorable position. I turned and
started in that direction.

As I turned, a Zero dove directly in front of me at close
range, apparently not seeing me. I gave a short burst that
must have been just right, for he exploded at once.

Before I could blink, a Grumman dove in front of me with
a Zero some distance behind, trying to get a shot. I fired,
but was so close I couldn't observe the effect. As he passed,
I looked around, however, and saw him burst into flames
and spin down. He didn't blow up.

Bate was off to my right with a Zero about a hundred
yards behind, pulling into a good position to shoot. When
the Zero was about five hundred feet below and shooting
at the Wildcat, I started firing. As my bullets crossed in
front of him, he pulled up and came at me head on, his guns
pumping.

By this time we were both firing, but neither of us registered. I still can't figure out how that happened. My tracers
were going over his hood; if they had been a few inches
lower, they would have brained him. His shots at me came
the same way. We were so close I could plainly see the pilot
and the green strip in front of the windshield to keep glare
out of his eyes. The cowling was bright red. We were curv-
ing around each other angrily, missing our targets by inches,

unable to find a proper angle to get hits. It was one of the most nerve-racking situations I was ever caught in.

He suddenly straightened out, climbed, made a turn around, and we came back at each other. He was above, coming down, and I was going up. Shooting head on, he made a right turn, giving me a chance to get on the inside. As I fired, it looked like my bullets were going into the side of his cockpit. I was off at a little angle.

His plane dove from 2,000 to 4,000 feet below me, made a big circle to the right and came back in my direction. I intended to go over and take another shot at him, but approaching Zeros changed my mind. Just as he passed me at about 100 yards, smoke started pouring out. By that time I was headed in the opposite direction toward a cloud. I kept watching, hoping fire would break out. When he was a half mile away, he burst into flames and started on down.

I dove into a cloud and traveled along its edges for some time to get my composure back. Emerging, I was directly in front of an approaching Wildcat. The pilot turned out to be Bate. We flew home in the rain. It got dark several miles from the field, so we had rain and darkness to make the trip in.

Bombs fell on the field as we were landing.

Everyone returned with the exception of Bill Marontate. He must have had a head on crash with an enemy plane. Before he went down, however, the other two boys with him, Presley and Bate, saw him shoot down one Zero. A gunner in a dive bomber said he saw him bail out safely. There were six other chutes in the air then, and all went down near the Jap destroyer. Our only hope is that Bill is a prisoner. His score was thirteen planes. He was a 4.0 man as well as a pilot.

I never expected to get out of that fight alive. Neither did Bate. "I consider myself a very lucky fellow," he remarked.

"A lot of lucky guys live around here," I pointed out.

The fighting that day was in the vicinity of New Georgia and Kolumbangara, 190 miles northwest of the field. Those three Zeros brought my score to twenty-six.

Other members of the flight got four more planes on the trip, making our total seventy-two. Hits were scored on the transport, setting it on fire.

CHAPTER XV

Y

THAT DAY'S FLARE-UP OF ACTION ON A FRONT LONG QUIET was obviously inspired by the Japanese necessity of reinforcing and supplying their troops on Guadalcanal. Our boys were beginning a steady advance, gaining 3,000 to 4,000 yards with each push. In four days they killed over 1,000 Japs.

Even Maytag Charlie was gone. Some of the AA boys trapped him in the beams of their searchlights one night and ended his seemingly magic life. Pilots and AA fire had downed 584 enemy planes against a loss of 180 American planes and 99 men up to this time.

Next day the Japs turned timid again. We went up to meet four Zeros, but they turned and ran up the channel before we could make contact.

General Geiger sent me a box of cigars with his compliments. Major Cram gave me two more boxes.

148

There was rain and more rain, which made it a bit wet.

Bill Freeman and Hap Hanson were down with malaria again.

Our strafing from the air made life miserable for Japs on the island. On dawn patrol I spotted a Jap truck and cut it to pieces. Next day I got a Jap machine-gun nest and some three-inch gunners on the beach. We made a wild goose chase to bomb ships but the weather closed in, preventing contact. We found a Jap supper fire in the rain and consoled ourselves by feeding them some hot lead for chow. Major Campbell found some Japs swimming in the river and gave them the hotfoot. Loesch discovered Japs washing clothes and purified the water for them. Presley caught one on a bridge and got him running. All minor doings—but they seemed like fun at the time.

Secretary of the Navy Frank Knox visited the island January 21. We gave him an escort that a Japanese armada could not have penetrated. The Japs apparently knew somebody important was around, because bombs started falling early and continued late. The field was bombed all night. I slept regardless of it.

I became known as operations officer every other day. The duties mostly involved answering the phone like a googoo girl and directing flights. The day started at 4:30 A.M. and ended when the last plane was in. It was confusing with seven telephones continually ringing.

Mechanics, the unsung heroes of the air wars, had a less hectic time these days and deserved it. In the first months on Guadalcanal they worked night and day to keep our planes in the air. When they slept, they rolled up in a blanket right under the planes. Without all the necessary tools, they were wonders at improvising.

Nobody can say anything against the grease monkeys when I'm around. Right up to the last, old 53, the plane I had flown onto Guadalcanal, was still in there with the best, although she had been shot full of holes many times. Her tail, both wings, and the back part of her fuselage was a collection of patches. The mechs had cut out the jagged holes left by cannon fire and the little round machine-gun holes. Then they had put on those countless patches. The motor itself had been replaced at least once that I knew of.

Several of these boys who maintained planes for my flight were killed by bombs, and others were wounded by shell fragments. The day that little Andy Andrews' plane went haywire, it killed one mechanic and injured another.

New flight strips had been added to Henderson Field by this time, and they could handle the heaviest and fastest bombers.

The boys went out after some Jap ships January 24 and got a hit on one after running into some Zeros, of which four were shot down. One dive bomber and two fighters failed to return.

When January 25 arrived, I knew it would be my last day at Guadalcanal and my last day of flying for a while. I also had a hunch there would be some excitement.

As we went on scramble stand-by at noon, I said, "We haven't left here yet, and we particularly want to be on the lookout today. Just because we're leaving is no reason we shouldn't pay attention to business and put on a show of shows today." The boys in the flight were the same except that for Marontate we had substituted Captain Philip White, of Syracuse, New York.

When they scrambled us at 12:45, we shot off the field, cut short, and at 180° from the field everyone was joined up tight. It was the best join-up I've ever seen or been in.

We climbed to the ceiling of 18,000 feet, circled, and were joined by four P-38s. As we moved out toward Savo Island we noticed twelve Zeros playing around, doing nip-ups and chasing each other.

"Okay, gang," I said, "let's go and get the so-and-sos." When we were within a mile of them, I noticed a hole in the overcast. Thinking it was funny for the Zeros to be playing around, I climbed to see what was above. There were about twenty more Zeros. Half a mile farther away were about twenty-four dive bombers, and behind them were more planes—I couldn't see what they were.

I went back down and said, "We aren't going out there. They want us to attack those Zeros so the gang above can send its dive bombers and fighter escort right to the field while we're busy. Let's stay tight formation and circle."

Two P-38s got on one side of the big circle and two on the other. We just moved around. Then the Japs sent over six Zeros, which circled temptingly, 1,000 to 2,000 feet below.

It was hard bait to resist. I actually started once, then thought, "Oh, yeah, we would go down to bust them off and then those other birds would have us away from the overcast."

"Just continue wheeling and keep your eyes on them," I radioed the boys. We could see Zeros above us break through the haze for an occasional peek to see where we were, then disappear in the overcast again. When they did that, I would change our course. We kept weaving back and forth, and every time they dove out, we were somewhere else. They kept hoping they would break out right behind us.

Finally the Japs below tired of circling without getting a nibble. Four of them went back to join the formation. The other two started up to our altitude. One climbed in front of me in ideal range. I could have shot him, but we just waited. One made a 180° turn and climbed within a hundred yards of Captain Loesch, but we just sat and looked at him, waiting for those dive bombers.

In the meantime a lot of our fighters were coming up. I had radioed the field long before—in short words too.

One of the Zeros, failing to see the P-38s, pulled in front of them so close the first two passed him. As he wiggled his wings and looked, the third riddled him at such close range it must have put powder burns on the back of the Jap's neck. He didn't explode but just burst into flames and went into a long dive into the sea near Savo.

The other Zero made a dive on the P-38 but our man just shoved down his throttle and gunned around. The nearest P-38 swung onto the Jap's tail, followed him into a cloud, and pretty soon sent him bouncing out, smoking like hell. Back went the P-38 into formation.

By that time the air was full of our fighters and the enemy was running short of gasoline. The dogs then turned and fled for home. Later I was told their force included eighteen high-level bombers too.

One of our flights below that day ran into twenty Zeros, got two, popped into the clouds, popped out, and got three more. The enemy raiders came from Bougainville and Munda.

We didn't get a shot that day. But we were satisfied—our teamwork had outwitted them and turned aside their Sunday punch. That was the last flight of the Flying Circus.

CHAPTER XVI

Υ

ON OUR TWO TRIPS TO THE ISLAND THE SQUADRON COMMANDED by Duke Davis knocked down one hundred and thirty-two Jap planes with the loss of fourteen pilots. My flight happened to get seventy-two of these planes. Nearly every boy in the Flying Circus wound up an ace—Marontate had thirteen victims, Loesch eight, Haberman seven, Freeman six, Presley five, Bate four, and Furlow three.

On January 26 we said our last good-byes and flew to Espiritu Santo, about 500 miles to the south. There I stayed with Jimmy Flatley, the Navy's expert on fighter tactics. We talked tactics by the hour.

I began to run into old friends—Lieutenant Jimmy Jacobson, a Marine raider from my home time; Ben Finney, and others. General Geiger and Major Cram took me on a one-day visit to another island.

We stayed at Espiritu Santo till February 17, and the days were pretty much the same. We luxuriated in the rest we got.

154

Mostly there was nothing new except the latest coconuts that had just dropped off.

We flew to New Caledonia, and five days later went to Auckland, New Zealand. There were conferences with generals occasionally, but for the most part I just loafed and ate the good food. I quit taking quinine and came down with a malaria relapse again.

We sailed for the United States at long last on March 25. With me were Bate, Furlow, Presley, Freeman, Haberman, and Loesch. Two days out at sea malaria bowled me over completely. Some of the boys gave me up for dead. I could hear a sailor griping about the canvas that would be wasted on my funeral at sea, but another fellow was howling even louder. He was the guy who would have had to sew me in.

I thought of the irony of dying at sea after escaping death so many times on Guadalcanal. But after four days, quinine snapped me out of it and I got up again, dizzier than a goat. I'm still taking quinine in small doses.

When we docked on the West Coast April 19 I immediately tried to call up my wife but found she was on the way to Washington, where I was expected. I went to San Diego in a station wagon, stayed there that night, and left the next noon for Washington by plane.

There I met my wife at last and plunged into a long series of conferences with high-ranking officials. I hadn't realized that there was anything very remarkable about shooting down twenty-six planes till I got to Washington.

I met General Holcomb, the Marine commandant; General Denig, head of Marine public relations; Secretary of the Navy Frank Knox; Ralph A. Bard, under-secretary of the Navy; Admiral King; Colonel Jerome, the man who first gave me the real itch to fly, and many others. I was put on nation-wide broadcasts and subjected to my first press conference. The newspapermen were very nice, and it was fun talking with them.

I went out to the Pentagon Building to give a lecture for Army Intelligence officers, and went to church Easter Sunday. I went to Quantico and gave more talks, running into Billy Ryan there. He was a football star at USD and is now with the FBI. I talked before the National Press Club, then went to Annapolis and addressed the upperclassmen at the naval academy. All this speaking was a little hard for a fellow who wasn't any orator and knew it. But everyone was very kind, and I thought if they could take it, I could too.

June and I went to New York, where we stayed in a big suite at the Waldorf-Astoria and saw something of the night life. One day I went out to the Grumman plant at Bethpage, Long Island, and talked before thousands of workers in a big assembly room from which the airplanes had been cleared. I got a kick out of meeting the men and women who built our Wildcats.

Then began a long swing over the country which the Marine Corps had arranged. First of all we headed for Sioux Falls.

The welcome I got there is something I'll remember all my life. I guess a fellow is concerned most of all about what the home folks think of him—I know I always was. In this city of 41,000 a crowd of 75,000 turned out that day. It was cold and cloudy and raw, and a harsh wind filled the air with grit. But it was a perfect day anyway. There was a lump in my throat as big as a pumpkin as I rode down the main street and heard the people cheer. The newspaper described that parade as the longest ever held in South Dakota.

I stayed there all week, with people almost trampling each other in efforts to do something for me. There were meetings, and armloads of gifts, and organizations that wanted me to be an honorary lifetime member. I've never seen anything like it.

It made me think of the days when I was going to school and working in Tolly's filling station. I decided then that we were going to be driven into war, and this was what led me into the Marine Corps. The Marines always get to see action. Maybe it was just a dumb guess, but in those days I told anybody who would listen that it would be the Japs who would attack us first.

After that week the tour was on, and I ran into deeply touching hospitality everywhere—Chicago, New York, Hartford, Connecticut, then Washington.

The return to Washington was for a special reason. I'd been tipped off in Chicago—I was to receive the Congressional Medal of Honor from President Roosevelt.

It was one of those experiences hard to talk about or describe. On May 18 I went to the White House with June and my mother. They had been invited to Washington especially for the occasion.

In the White House lobby we met Generals Holcomb and Geiger, and they took us into the office of General Watson, one of the President's aides. Pretty soon Cordell Hull and Frank Knox came in, accompanied by ex-Governor Lehman of New York. They talked and laughed, but I didn't say much. Then Secretary Hull went out. "I hope you live another hundred years," he told me.

After fifteen or twenty minutes we went into the President's office. Wearing a rumpled seersucker suit, he was seated at his desk—the one I'd seen in all the newsreels. He shook hands all around. Then he remarked that he had something for me.

He picked up the citation from his desk and read it while I stood there, embarrassed. The citation went like this:

For outstanding heroism and courage above and beyond the call of duty as executive officer of Marine Fighting Squadron 121, at Guadalcanal, Solomon Islands. Engaging in almost daily combat with the enemy from October 9 to November 19, 1942, Captain Foss personally shot down 23 Japanese planes and damaged others so severely that their destruction was extremely probable. In addition, during this period he successfully led a large number of escort missions, skillfully covering reconnaissance, bombing and photographic planes as well as surface craft. On January 15, 1943, he added three more enemy planes to his already brilliant successes for a record of aerial combat achievement unsurpassed in this war. Boldly searching out an approaching enemy force on January 25, Captain Foss led his eight F4F marine planes and four army P-38s into action and, undaunted by tremendously superior numbers, intercepted and struck with such force that four Japanese fighters were shot down and the bombers were turned back without releasing a single bomb. His remarkable flying skill, inspiring leadership and indomitable fighting spirit were distinctive factors in the defense of strategic American positions on Guadalcanal.

> Franklin D. Roosevelt.
> President, United States.

Then he asked me to step over beside him. He also asked June to come over and help. I leaned down. He put the medal around my neck and June snapped the clasp in back.

The President smiled and said he guessed we'd have to do it over again so all the cameramen would have a chance.

After thanking him, we started out. Secretary Knox remarked that I was one of the boys who escorted him when he visited Guadalcanal. Then we left.

I picked up the tour again, visiting, among other places, Newark, Chapel Hill, Jacksonville, Pensacola, Eglin Field, New Orleans, Corpus Christi, Los Angeles, San Diego, San Francisco, Del Monte, and St. Mary's Preflight School.

At Chicago I had seen Haberman, and at Newark, where I visited the near-by Curtiss-Wright plant, Bate showed up. In New York they took me to the "I Am An American" celebration, where more than a million people were gathered. I gave a short talk, and Mayor LaGuardia asked me some questions.

In one day at New York I almost lost my voice from making twenty-four speeches.

One day I got word that I had been promoted to major. About the same time, the grapevine brought news that most of my boys had been made captains. It was good to hear of that.

In the East I ran into red-haired Ralph Gunvordahl, who hitchhiked to Minneapolis with me in the winter of 1940 to join the Marines. He's a test pilot for Eastern Aircraft at Linden, New Jersey, now.

There were other bits of news here and there—some of it good, some bad. Lieutenant John Maas got the Distinguished Flying Cross. Those crack Australian aces I'd met at Sydney were killed by Japs over Darwin. I saw some of the new planes that'll be coming up pretty soon, and they're bad news for the Germans and Japs. There were long distance phone calls, letters, and personal visits with parents of boys who had been killed. The courage with which these mothers and fathers took their loss was infinitely fine. They are certainly true Americans.

I learned that Eddie Rickenbacker had generously sent me his congratulations, away back in February. I never got his letter. Somebody must have copped it for a souvenir.

Right now the Marine Corps thinks I'm of more value as a tactical adviser than as a fighter pilot. It will be all right for a few months. I'd like to get a good rest and get rid of the malaria bugs for once and all. Then I want to be in there again somewhere, shooting those good .50-caliber guns and working the controls of a hot military airplane. That's the life for me till this war is over.

RETURN TO the circulation desk of any
University of California Library
or to the

NORTHERN REGIONAL LIBRARY FACILITY
Bldg. 400, Richmond Field Station
University of California
Richmond, CA 94804-4698

ALL BOOKS MAY BE RECALLED AFTER 7 DAYS
2-month loans may be renewed by calling
(415) 642-6753
1-year loans may
to N
Renew
prio

JUN